Computer Games and the Social Imaginary

Digital Media and Society Series

Nancy Baym: *Personal Connections in the Digital Age*
Jean Burgess and Joshua Green: *YouTube*
Mark Deuze: *Media Work*
Andrew Dubber: *Radio in the Digital Age*
Charles Ess: *Digital Media Ethics 2nd edition*
Alexander Halavais: *Search Engine Society*
Martin Hand: *Ubiquitous Photography*
Robert Hassan: *The Information Society*
Tim Jordan: *Hacking*
Graeme Kirkpatrick: *Computer Games and the Social Imaginary*
Leah Lievrouw: *Alternative and Activist New Media*
Rich Ling and Jonathan Donner: *Mobile Communication*
Donald Matheson and Stuart Allan: *Digital War Reporting*
Dhiraj Murthy: *Twitter*
Zizi Papacharissi: *A Private Sphere*
Jill Walker Rettberg: *Blogging 2nd edition*
Patrik Wikström: *The Music Industry 2nd edition*

Computer Games and the Social Imaginary

G RAEME K IRKPATRICK

polity

First published in 2013 by Polity Press

Polity Press
65 Bridge Street
Cambridge CB2 1UR, UK

Polity Press
350 Main Street
Malden, MA 02148, USA

ISBN-13: 978-0-7456-4110-2
ISBN-13: 978-0-7456-4111-9(pb)

A catalogue record for this book is available from the British Library.

Typeset in 10.25 on 13 pt Scala
by Toppan Best-set Premedia Limited
Printed and bound in Great Britain by Berforts Information Press Ltd

The publisher has used its best endeavours to ensure that the URLs for external websites referred to in this book are correct and active at the time of going to press. However, the publisher has no responsibility for the websites and can make no guarantee that a site will remain live or that the content is or will remain appropriate.

Every effort has been made to trace all copyright holders, but if any have been inadvertently overlooked the publisher will be pleased to include any necessary credits in any subsequent reprint or edition.

For further information on Polity, visit our website: www.politybooks.com

For Sarah

Contents

Acknowledgements   viii

Introduction   1

Chapter 1: Computer Games in Social Theory   9
1. Gaming and the Social Imaginary   14
2. The Gamer as a 'Streamlined Self'   21
3. Social Theory and Critique   27

Chapter 2: Lineages of the Computer Game   38
1. The Revival of Play   40
2. Technology and the Dialectic of Invention   49
3. Artistic Critique and the Transformation
    of Computing   61

Chapter 3: The Formation of Gaming Culture   70
1. The Discovery of 'Gameplay'   74
2. The 'Authentic' Gamer   81
3. Gaming's Constitutive Ambivalence   91

Chapter 4: Technology and Power   98
1. Organizing an Industry   101
2. Globalization and the Cultures of Production   109
3. Technology, Power and Resistance   118

Chapter 5: The Phenakisticon   128
1. MMPGs in Recognition-Theoretic Perspective   131
2. The Limitations of Engineered Sociability   139
3. Ludefaction and the Diminution of Gameplay   150

Chapter 6: Aesthetics and Politics   159
1. The Aesthetic Dimension   163
2. Art, Play and Critique   170
3. Critical Gaming?   175

Notes   188
References   201
Index   215

Acknowledgements

I would like to thank Andrea Drugan and Lauren Mulholland of Polity Press for their patience, support and encouragement at various points in the writing of this book. The book could not have been written without the kindness and intellectual generosity of friends and fellow scholars in the game studies community. Andreas Gregersen, Velli-Matti Karhulahti, Olli Tapio Leino and Feng Zhu gave selflessly of their time to read and comment on extensive portions of the manuscript and they each made many helpful suggestions. I haven't been able to incorporate all of their ideas but, thanks to them, the book is much better now than it was before.

I am grateful to the following people for their encouragement, support and some fascinating conversations that have influenced my thinking while I've been working on this project: Andrew Feenberg, Espen Aarseth, Piotr Sitarski, Nick Crossley, Mike Savage, Christian Ulrik Andersen, Jonas Linderoth, Staffan Björk, Helen Kennedy, Cheryl Martens, Steve Hall, Andrew McCulloch, Bo Kampmann Walther, Charles Ess, Melanie Swalwell, Andreas Lange, Jakko Suominen, Petri Saarikoski, Yoni Van den Eede, Simon Niedenthal, Ann Cronley, Martin Watkins, Gareth Crabtree, Paul Brown, Eliah Tupou, Adam Trela, Ashley Brown and Gagun Chhina.

I would also like to thank Andy 'Roy' Holmes, who let me play games on his home computer in the 1980s, helping me to overcome various prejudices and phobias in the process. I am grateful to Theodor Araby-Kirkpatrick for his criticisms, numerous examples and distinctive outlook on life. This book is dedicated to my wife, Sarah Carling.

Introduction

Computer games and the distinctive culture that is associated with them are beginning to receive the attention they deserve from social theorists and sociologists.[1] This book argues that closer attention to games and gaming adds an important dimension to our understanding of society and contemporary culture more widely. Computer games have played a central role in the development of the digital technologies that are widely acknowledged to have transformed the global economy over the past four decades. They were central to the emergence of personal computers, to the diffusion of easy-to-use interfaces on technologies, and to the rise of the internet and the naturalizing of our experience of 'virtual' space. The spread and popularity of computer games can also be seen as a consequence of these developments but, I will argue, they exist in a complex and intimate interaction with the digital society and culture we now take for granted and they have shaped the world we live in.

In addition to the relatively obvious technological associations between gaming and other important forces in contemporary society, gaming is also exemplary in relation to fundamental social and cultural processes. Many of the changes to the commodity form in the age of digital downloads and 'interactivity' are most clearly exemplified by games. As Scott Lash and Celia Lury put it, 'the global culture industry is what happens when movies become games' (2007: 9). Moreover, the gaming industry has played a leading role in developing new working practices and applications of technology that have become definitive of the modern organization in networked capitalism. Computer games have been instrumental in the transformation of modern consumption and production processes, and in the development of practices that increasingly efface the distinction between the two.

This book is written from the perspective of a reflexive tradition in sociology, which starts from the principle that society is unlike other objects of our experience in that it is itself a social product. In other words, in order for us to really live 'in' a society, we must first believe that we do. We can only believe this because it is true, but that truth is contingent upon our already living out certain kinds of connection to others and our common possession of a shared way of understanding the world, including some notion of social space, in which those connections are established. The category of the social imaginary is essential to what follows. It refers to the background sense-making operations that make the idea of society and its practical reality possible. As Charles Taylor puts it, 'the social imaginary is not a set of "ideas", rather it is what enables, through making sense of, the practice of a society' (Taylor 2004: 2). The idea of an imagined community, which becomes a real one when we all think about it in the same way and act 'as if' it were really there, rests upon this creative capacity for imagining and instituting the social that defines us as humans.[2]

A central and in many ways troubling development of recent times concerns the relationship between the social imaginary and various technological media. As Lash and Lury point out, the social imaginary is a 'virtual' property: we have it in common and it is necessary to our experience of the world, but we cannot measure it or locate it empirically. At its heart is play, especially the play of ideas and concepts. This is, of course, an essential point of connection to computer games, and I take it to be indicative of their importance to contemporary culture and society. The character of our play is profoundly telling in relation to the character of our society. Luc Boltanski (2011) raises the question of what happens when social reality is so overwhelmingly flexible, when we are so saturated with ideas and experiences from the outside that we can no longer 'think against' the world because the world won't stand still long enough for us to get a good view of it. He suggests that contemporary social reality is too 'viscous' in this way for us to exercise our creativity, to bring about social change. Computer games are both a sign of this situation, confirming its reality, and a tool with which to think our way through it.

To do this we need to take a historical approach to computer games, in order to identify the reconfigurations they have brought about and to place these in their proper context. Computer games have shaped and been shaped in a dialogue with the rest of culture and this book attempts to trace out the key moments in this conversation. This book describes three intersections of gaming technology with mainstream computer design and technology change, each corresponding to a shift in the way that we conceive 'society'. The first is the development of user-friendly, easy-to-use computers, which changed the status and meaning of computers and technology from the late 1980s onwards. The transformation of computers which happened at this time has changed the popular understanding of what technology is and of what it can be, and established new rules for making sense of technology as a part of our collective envisioning of the social as an assemblage of practices and objects. Broadly speaking, prior to this shift, technology was productive tools and as such it was hard and efficient, but since the change machines have become objects of desire associated with play and adventure. The second intersection concerns the innovations in gaming in 1994–5, associated especially with *Doom* (1994) and *Myst* (1994). These coincided with the development of the World Wide Web into something culturally mainstream, again associated with changes to usability promoted by the Mosaic and then Netscape browsers. Here, games clearly drive the 'cyberspace' metaphor and are integral to the emergence of ideas, many of them utopian at first, about cyber or virtual society as a kind of new frontier, or an extension of established social space. Finally, and most recently, games have played an important role in promoting the metaphor and idea of the 'social network', as denoting ideas of connection under a horizon that makes the formation and maintenance of social ties into essentially ludic practices. Here, the way we process and make sense of the reflexive processes of relationship formation are being reconfigured, with implications for how we conceive and make sense of social experience.

The book begins with a further elaboration of the theoretical questions and concepts that motivate the enquiry, starting with the idea of the social imaginary itself. The kind of society that has shaped games and been shaped by them is portrayed, with particular reliance on Boltanski and Chiapello's (2005) thesis of a 'new spirit of capitalism'. According to that analysis, capitalism has taken advantage of computer and network technology to overhaul its core processes, especially in the sphere of work and management. The bureaucratic and industrial model of production has given way to a flexible system that is horizontally integrated. Instead of being managed from above, workers take responsibility for their own role in creative processes. Increasingly work is creative but it is also economically insecure. Individuals in developed economies face competition for most jobs, not just from local markets but from around the world as increasingly production is located in the 'virtual' space of electronic networks. The labour process is more of an 'adventure' but it also places demands on inner resources of each individual that were previously withheld from the economic sphere. This situation calls forth a new kind of economic subject, namely the 'streamlined worker', who is less concerned with developing a career than she is with playing the game well from day to day.

The origins of these changes lie in the counter-cultural movement of the late 1960s, which Boltanski and Chiapello characterize as offering an 'artistic critique' of old-fashioned capitalism and its associated 'culture industry'. Chapter 2 explores the origins of the computer game, one thread of which traces to a technophilic strain within that culture. This chapter examines the culture of play that existed prior to the eruption of games, looking at the history of play and toys in modern societies and at specific kinds of entertainment that also framed the development of the new form. In this way it emphasizes the contingency of computer games on a number of social and cultural factors. There was nothing inevitable about the creation of computer games and their existence was not 'technologically determined'. Rather, the actions of specific social groups in the US, Japan and Europe determined that our tinkering with complex digital artefacts should take the form of a game in the sense that we now take for granted. There is what Michael Chanan (1996) calls a 'dialectic of invention' between these cultural forces and the expanding capacities of digital technology, and the first games reflect the outcome of this complex interaction.

Chapter 3 describes the formation of a computer gaming culture through the prism of early computer and gaming magazines. It draws on some theoretical ideas from Pierre Bourdieu to present gaming as a cultural field with its own, specialized discourse. A new way of talking about games and appraising them was developed in connection with games played on home computers in the UK and Europe in the early 1980s. For those who internalized this discourse and made it the rationale for their own preferences and behaviours, it entered and informed their identity. Becoming a 'gamer' is a means of securing validation for one's activities and recognition from a group of peers. As such, gaming is recuperative for individuals. Learning to evaluate games and becoming an exponent of good 'gameplay' are the key to a certain kind of authenticity; to action in accordance with standards that are beyond manipulation by larger economic forces and may occasionally create friction between people who play the games and the companies that make them. At the same time, however, the chapter notes that gaming discourse falters in its attempt to establish fully autonomous criteria for game evaluation. In the fumbling inarticulacy of 1990s game reviews, we can see that gaming culture is marked by a series of constitutive ambivalences. Computer games are more than just games, but they do not become art; gaming is pleasurable and harmless yet also 'addictive' and, on occasion, 'not normal', and, finally, games are not suitable for children, yet they continue to be fundamentally childish. These tensions are constitutive for gaming culture and they become definitive for games and for their cultural position in a wider sense.

It is forlorn to expect, therefore, that gaming and gamers might be the locus of radical, politically conscious, oppositional movements and campaigns. Although games are things to be played, this play does not extend or update the 1960s idea of 'playpower' as an anti-capitalist value. Rather, gaming culture represents the status of play and games *after* the artistic critique has had its effects and caused its displacements. In so far as this culture does impose itself in an oppositional sense, this is nearly always through its demands for more problematic and contentious games. Chapter 4 describes how the revival of console gaming since the late 1980s involves a series of strategies aimed at managing the production of 'safe' commodities for a community that demands the non-safe, the provocative and, on occasion, the downright silly. This chapter explores changes to the production-side technologies of this time, especially the growth of middleware, or game engine technologies. These automate and de-skill the game production process and make it possible to relocate the labour of game production to virtual space, all of which impact negatively on workers in the industry. They also result, however, in games that feel similar to play because they deploy identical routines regardless of ostensible variation between games at the level of on-screen, or fictional content. In consequence, struggles arise between gamers and the industry on which they depend. Player demands for more cheeky, violent and troublesome games should be understood in this light. They are interpreted here in terms of the values that circulate among gamers as an imagined community, values which are knowing and cynical rather than progressive or articulated to wider social concerns.

Chapter 5 resumes the theme of play and games as recuperative for streamlined individuals, addressing the question of the concrete forms of alternative social life that have sprung up in 'massive multi-player on-line games' (MMPGs). Drawing on Axel Honneth's (1995) 'recognition-theoretic' approach to social relations, the chapter argues that social relationships formed in MMPGs are skewed by the limitations individuals accept when they enter ludic environments. Assuming a role in these games involves embracing a particular character-type, which carries limitations on the kinds of action people can perform in the game. This in turn affects the kind of recognition that can be secured there, which is partial and distorted. The phenakisticon (deceptive image) of the MMPG makes it impossible to reach sound conclusions about people's motivations, including one's own. This is true even despite the fact that we often know 'who' our fellow players are – it is not their identity that is in question but their (and our) reasons for being there. This is the sociological context in which we should interpret recent claims for a 'ludification' of contemporary society and culture, for while it may be true that ludic principles now permeate more areas of personal and collective life, these principles, and especially the character of the play they involve, have themselves altered in the process. The contemporary game of life is less a matter of ludification than of ludefaction – a corrosion of the creative powers of play.

The final chapter turns to an examination of the subjective impact of play with computer games. Games with screens and controllers stretch our sensoria and play with our habituated responses and expectations. The widespread embrace of such ostensibly quite unsettling experiences is perhaps the most interesting thing about the spread of computer games. Changes to our collective sensibility brought about by playing games constitute one of the most enduring consequences of the 'artistic critique' of technology and culture. Drawing on some ideas from Jacques Rancière (Tanke 2012), this chapter explores the contrast between computer games and art. The book concludes by comparing the experiences of what Rancière calls 'subjectivation' in connection with the two forms. The ambivalence of computer games, analysed in earlier chapters, here bears quite bitter fruit, but it probably opens up more questions than it answers, especially as regards the future potential of the form. I argue, nonetheless, that it is in their aesthetic aspect that computer games hold most interest for critical theorists. Assessing them from this perspective affords us the clearest view on their social and cultural significance.

CHAPTER ONE

Computer Games in Social Theory

The aim of this book is to provide a clearer understanding of the cultural importance of the computer game. Computer games have been with us for a long time. They started out as the preserve of a small group of technological enthusiasts and hobbyists and became a multinational industry. In a strange way, this happened twice. At the end of the 1970s the industry grew rapidly and took on international proportions, only to fall back dramatically in the early 1980s. Since the mid-1980s computer games have become a global culture industry with projected annual turnover for 2013 of around $70 billion. It is claimed that computer games have become culturally mainstream, that everyone plays them regardless of age and gender, and that they are part of a new social and cultural reality with political import (McGonigal 2011).

The years in which the computer game has developed have been decades of rapid and momentous transformation, associated with phrases like 'the information revolution' and 'globalization'. Digital technologies including games have changed the fundamental principles of social and economic organization so that we see new goods as well as old ones produced and distributed in completely new ways. These technologies have changed our ways of creating and communicating, so that scientific practices, the arts and the media all now move to a different rhythm than before. Networked computing has reconfigured our understanding of society and our understanding of our own contribution to social life. 'Social media' like Facebook are a very clear illustration of how the very practices of social interaction have been drastically altered by the salience of digital devices and the reality of digital connection. These kinds of changes affect the very meaning of 'society'.

The computer game[1] has played a central role in helping people to navigate these changes. It has been instrumental in introducing many people to computer technologies and in making the use of digital devices habitual and intuitive. At the same time, the computer game has been shaped by its historical context. The idea of playing games with a computer was not a natural occurrence – it reflected the outcome of cultural activity and social choices. Both these processes are ongoing: computer games continue to leverage changes and cultural innovations and they are constantly being re-shaped by the environment in which they operate. This book tries to map the implication of computer games in many of the changes of the last 30–40 years and to identify how shifts in the social and cultural environment have shaped the games that we play.

The project of the book, then, is to position the computer game and gaming as a cultural practice in a theory of contemporary society. The rationale for such an undertaking is clear. Computer games matter because a lot of people play them and because they occupy a place of great strategic significance in the culture. Social theorists, I submit, need to think about the issues raised by gaming. For example, there has been much discussion recently about the role of social media in promoting new forms of political action and a new more engaged citizenry (Morozov 2010; Joyce 2010).[2] Gamers are an important section of any new public identified in those terms – playing games is something most people do when they join the growing number of the world's population who use networked computers regularly. If we all play games now, it is important to understand how they fit into our lives and affect the other roles that we have as individuals in society. In what follows I will try to show the role computer games play in reconfiguring notions that have framed our understanding of ourselves and our relation to the society we live in.

Aphra Kerr has pointed out that a social history of games 'would focus less on dates and inventors and more on struggles and uncertainties' (Kerr 2006: 20). I have tried to observe this principle in the chapters that follow. Writing in ostensibly similar tones, Nick Dyer-Witheford and Greig de Peuter have offered a highly politicized 'account that explores virtual games within a system of global ownership, privatized property, coercive class relations, military operations and radical struggle' (2009: xxix). In contrast, however, this book attempts the more modest task of explaining how computer games have claimed the position they now occupy in contemporary culture. This involves focusing on struggles waged on behalf of the new medium to secure its recognition as a valid pastime. A first set of relevant struggles, then, concerns the effort to make games that appeal to children *and* parents in a context where parents are told that games are bad for their children and children embrace games partly because parents vaguely disapprove of them. Or the struggle to make games for games' sake, in a context where those managing the production process are only really concerned with efficiency and marketability. Or the struggle to get games that people can enjoy playing *together* in a society of increasingly isolated individuals, in which social atomization is often attributed to things like computer games. These are the social struggles that mark the development of the computer game as a cultural form and they are a primary focus of this book.

These struggles, in which the computer game finds itself and wins its cultural presence, so to speak, have wider entanglements. The fact that families incorporate the computer game in all its ambivalence into their homes, for example, connects to wider questions, and touches on long-established distinctions through which we have sorted and made sense of the social world, like the public–private distinction and the difference between production and consumption. The fact that public technology enters the home and permeates intimate relationships is an important social fact related to the historical transformations mentioned above. Similarly, the fact that people associate digital devices with play has implications for the way they relate to their working tools. The apparent blurring of work and play here expresses profound changes in the way that society is organized, including key productive processes. Games have been agents in the transformation of what we might call the aesthetics of technology – what machines feel like to use – and this marks an abrupt and important break in recent social history. It is essential to understand the role played by games in the wider struggles associated with these and other transitions.

These issues are addressed in the chapters that follow. This chapter begins by concentrating on three central topics of contemporary social theory within which the computer game occupies an important place. We start with the bigger picture, by locating computer games within the wider transformations associated with globalization and what has been called the 'new spirit of capitalism' (Boltanski and Chiapello 2005). This sets the scene for detailed exploration of the social processes that shaped the first computer games, which are the focus of the next chapter, and those through which games and gaming have won the cultural location they currently occupy, which is the theme of chapter 3.

The key concepts in this chapter are the social imaginary and a new kind of subjectivity specific to digital culture, described by Boltanski and Chiapello (2005) as the 'streamlined' individual. The chapter begins by defining the idea of the social imaginary in more detail and identifying the relationship of the idea to the history of technological media. Section 1 shows how a specific permutation of the social imaginary associated with print technology was fundamental to the development of modern, democratic societies. It then goes on to discuss the negative impact of twentieth-century 'mass media' on democratic culture in terms of a constriction of the creative powers of the social imaginary, before offering some first thoughts on how computer games might break with this.

The next section turns to the question of the individual who believes in and participates in the co-creation of this re-configured social space. Social theorists have argued that contemporary individuals experience crises of identity related especially to the rhythms of life imposed by the demands of the new economic situation associated with globalization. They focus on the discrepancy between these and the idea of a coherent self with a biography that 'makes sense'. Here the 'gamer' identity is pivotal, combining as it does aspects that reflect functional adjustment to the new situation with the opportunity to bolster and reinforce personal identity in a new cultural practice. The gaming self is equipped to participate in the new economy but also has access to remedial cultural resources that compensate us for the new kinds of vulnerability associated with that participation.

Finally, the chapter turns to the issue of critique and the usefulness of social theory in the circumstances described here. The purpose of critique is to identify niches, points in contemporary experience where individuals and groups might find a foothold from which they can enhance their own leverage over the situations in which they find themselves. Rather than being swept along with the flow of an increasingly 'viscous' (Boltanksi 2011) social reality that demands narrow pursuit of one's own interests, critique exposes points at which action based on deliberation and reflection might lead to an opening for ideas that contribute to the general well-being of society. This is not a top-down operation, in which the expert transmits the truth to a grateful reader, but rather a dialogue in which historical and other ideas are introduced into conversations and practices that are already ongoing. The onus is on the author to identify these conversations and to make appropriately targeted interventions and suggestions.

One of the purposes of this book is to try and identify such points within gaming as a cultural practice.

1. Gaming and the Social Imaginary

Regardless of their historical circumstances, people have to be able to think the nature of the social collective they participate in. This thinking necessarily involves an imaginative dimension, which cannot be separated from quantitative or physical descriptions. We know that we are 'in' a society, but what that means to us is historically and culturally variable, and, while the strictly physical correlates of the idea are essential, they are indeterminate. Rather, the popular conception of society is made up out of images, ideas and impressions which, in Castoriadis' (1987) phrase, 'lean on' more literal descriptive accounts of relevant social quanta. These two dimensions are inseparable and interdependent. Castoriadis refers to a kind of 'magma' of uninterpreted material that conditions how we make sense of the social world and how we position the resulting idea of society in understanding our own experience.[3] Describing social phenomena involves creative interpretation and a play of our descriptive resources and capacities: it is never determined, only conditioned by this magma. There are, therefore, rules of sense-making that we use from day to day and which maintain the notion of a society in which we live. The social imaginary is where we find these rules and the margin for interpretative play and innovation that is dubbed the 'radical imaginary' by Castoriadis. It is particularly important to notice that even when it seems to us as if society is dominated and determined by forces beyond our control, the imaginary dimension has given rise to that interpretation and that way of thinking about them. Social events are always constituted out of interpretations acted upon and this reflexivity is ineliminable and all-pervasive. The idea of events as determined and determinate is, in fact, an effect of reflexive-interpretative processes that, if understood, would falsify the idea: the social magma is real but indeterminate.

The factors that most affect our specific historical experience of the social imaginary are the communications media through which we share and distribute ideas in a social register. It was media technology, especially print, that established the 'imagined communities' (Anderson 1985) that made people believe they were living in modern societies in which they had a role to play as citizens. Key sources here are John B. Thompson's (1995) study of the media and modernity and Jürgen Habermas' (1989) idea of print culture as providing 'launching-off points' for the modern public sphere. Moveable type technology, developed in the fifteenth century, inaugurated a series of historical events that culminated in what theorists call the public sphere. The production and circulation of printed information changed how people imagined the wider social world, from a situation in which local, proximal factors determined their sense of who they were and what they could do, to one in which identification with distant others became more important. Social activity now took place in imagined spaces they shared with others, both as reference points for action and as sources of identity. The modern self is one that develops through engagement with and participation in a new kind of space that is detached from place. This space is the primary effect of the 'modern social imaginary' (Taylor 2004); it is the reality that underpins popular discourse on society and it accommodates the structures and unities that are studied by sociology.

Modern societies are democratic because the use of print as a medium of integration creates the possibility that people can recognize themselves as agents in the creation of social life, as participants on the same terms as everyone else who reads the papers. In this way, the modern social imaginary involves a subjective, psychological orientation that is essential to being a free and equal citizen. Habermas (1989) identifies the psychological novel of the eighteenth century as a launching-off point for the public sphere as a space that is uncoupled from place and in which people come together to agree on the rules of social co-existence. Often epistolary in form, these novels offered readers rich portrayals of the inner lives of others with whom they could identify as being 'like them' and as sharing a common social horizon. In the public sphere, reason, debate and the struggle for mutual comprehension hold sway rather than money and power, which also rapidly developed new potency and new forms of operation in the eighteenth and nineteenth centuries (Habermas 1989). For Habermas, the tension between these two dimensions of social evolution defines the modern period.

The public sphere represents the strongest possibility for a society in which reason and debate can determine the forms of social organization, liberating people from naked domination by the powerful or by the drudgery that Karl Marx called the 'dull compulsion of the economic' (Marx 1990). Communications media, and especially the print revolution, are at the centre of the idea. Thompson (1995) clarifies the importance of media with reference to three factors. First, media provide symbolic resources with which we can collectively fashion a social imaginary. Once people are exposed to media, the range of symbolic meanings they can draw on to construct an image of society becomes greatly expanded. Second, this influx of symbols is related to communicative action, which now enjoys occupancy of the new space. Reading documents produced in Brussels in my home in Yorkshire and knowing that other people are reading the same words in Berlin greatly enlarges my sense of the space that I, and others like me, occupy. This space is populated by the exchange of ideas, and communicative practices give it meaning and form (consider the resonances of the idea of 'Europe'). Finally, involvement in these processes involves a new sense of self. As I relate to others and to space on new terms, so I become a different kind of being. The modern sense of self is no longer rooted in 'the familiar and the routine' (Thompson 1995: 189) – as individuals are aware of more 'alternatives to existing practices'.

The rise of modern communications media, then, is experienced as liberating. It frees people from the ties of tradition, exposes them to new ideas and creates a new space in which they can participate as citizens. At the same time, however, it creates a new kind of dependency. As Thompson puts it, 'the more the process of self-formation is enriched by mediated symbolic forms, the more the self becomes dependent on media systems which lie beyond its control' (1995: 214).

According to Habermas, this dependency becomes pathological in the twentieth century. The critical social theorists of the Frankfurt School, with which Habermas was associated (Held 1989; Jay 1973), argued that culture as a whole in the post-Second World War period became industrialized, in the dual sense that it subserved capitalist industry and acquired an industrial production logic of its own. Studies of the 'culture industry' by Theodor Adorno, Max Horkheimer and other members of the Frankfurt School emphasized the homogeneity of cultural production in the mid-twentieth century. 'Films, radio and magazines', wrote Adorno and Horkheimer, 'make up a system which is uniform as a whole and in every part' (Adorno and Horkheimer 1997: 120).

Behind this system lurk corporate interests that seek to manipulate people and render them docile and compliant. Critically, the media are being used not simply to distract people, but to make them into consumers, whose desires and wants are effectively tailored to the needs of a cyclical, capitalist economy. The products of the culture industry are shallow reflections of what is. They encourage identification with the present as 'normal' and restrict our sense of what is possible. Watching a soap opera, you do not come away with ideas about how things might be made better, but with your sense of the normalcy of contemporary social relations reinforced. Your thirst for something other than mundane, repetitive life dominated by social demands that are construed as irresistible and determinate is unaddressed and your real desires remain repressed. For Adorno and Horkheimer (1997), this repression has a physiognomic dimension: the workers who fed off the culture industry were physically exhausted and all too ready to slump in their armchairs in front of TV football or the latest formulaic serial.

Drawing on these analyses by his Frankfurt forebears, Habermas was pessimistic about the prospects for the public sphere in the twentieth century, mainly because of the impact of broadcast media on rational deliberative processes. As Adorno (1994) wrote in his analysis of the astrology columns in a 1950s newspaper, the products of the culture industry prey on the fact that their audiences are incapable of the kind of independence of mind, or personal autonomy, needed for active participation in civic life. Rather, they crave relief from the burden of this failure, which the astrology column and other culture industry products provide even as they intensify and aggravate the underlying condition. The dependent readers are encouraged to see themselves as independent, so long as they follow the advice given to them by a completely ridiculous source: a newspaper astrologer. Above all they are admonished to 'Think positively, be extrovert and have fun!' Adorno writes that,

> The individual is promised the solution to everything if he complies with certain requirements and avoids certain negative stereotypes. He is prevented from really acknowledging the very same difficulties which drive him into the arms of astrology. (1994: 65)

In this way, a real responsibility – to be rational, autonomous and to participate as a citizen – is removed and replaced with the more manageable one of appearing to be happy with the demands placed on us by society:

> One is forced to have fun in order to be well adjusted or at least appear so to others because only well-adjusted people

are accepted as normal and are likely to be successful. (1994: 75)

Advice in the astrology columns involved things like the instruction not to 'sulk' over 'disappointing acts' by 'an influential executive'. The reader is counselled to disregard their true feelings in the pursuit of appearing to be 'normal' and enjoying professional success. The astrology column exemplifies how products of the culture industry closed down the margin of the radical imaginary and made each individual responsible for his or her own adjustment to a social reality that demanded compliance (Adorno 1994: 59).

Digital media technology have transformed this situation, primarily because they require us to be active, to participate and to connect with others as part of their functioning. Computer games have been fundamental to this change. As we will see further in the next chapter, games were from the outset social in their orientation. The first computer games were produced with groups of players in mind. Games like *Spacewar!* (1962) and *Adventure* (1975) were made to be shared within communities of programming enthusiasts (the first computer 'hackers'). Moreover, this playful orientation to computers contributed to the idea of trying to get the machines to talk to each other. In other words, gaming was an important driver behind the development of networked computing – it was not something that got tacked on as an afterthought. Even in its earliest phase, computer gaming involved this positive social orientation. Computer games are also at odds with the physiognomic characterization of culture industry products. They do not tolerate passivity but demand active participation by players, simply because without player activity there is no game. In this way they also produce new experiences of space. Here, the spaces are primarily those of play itself: in living rooms all over the world the visual space of television is drawn out and incorporated into the minds and bodies of players. The frenetic activities of players' hands and bodies are only interpretable on the basis of imagined events taking place in game space. Here, and through developments like mobile and pervasive gaming, gamers use technology to re-fashion their immediate environments, infusing them with new symbolic contents and alternative structures that support activities – including playful competitions, races, puzzles and team games – that are only possible because players share the same ideas and, in acting on those ideas, they confer a specific reality on them (Walther 2005).

In Scott Lash and Celia Lury's (2007) study of contemporary media culture, they define the social imaginary as a kind of 'collective memory' that stands between our empirical experience and more abstract, or rationalized, ideas about the social world. They emphasize that the idea is neither purely public in the sense of being embodied in an anonymous structure, nor merely a property of individual minds. Rather, it is what they call 'a virtual' on the grounds that it lacks coordinates in the empirical world and yet is constantly being instantiated in social experience. They emphasize the positive implications of a more playful relationship with commodities for the social imaginary.[4] A defining feature of contemporary commodities is that they involve a 'provocation to play':

> the objects of the global culture industry tantalise our capacity to deal with wholes and parts, continuity and discontinuity, synchrony and succession. They extend and disrupt the space and time in which we move. They are the media of flow, a culture of circulation in which we are entangled, sometimes snared. (Lash and Lury 2007: 152)

In what they call the 'global culture industry', Lash and Lury argue that the situation is both worse and better than the one described by Adorno and Horkheimer. It is worse because now individuals are far more dependent on the objects they are involved in. We define ourselves more than ever through our purchases and our gadgets. But things are also better because through those objects we reflexively co-participate in the production of new experiences. The contemporary revival and rehabilitation of play and its entanglement with commodities presents possibilities of being 'drawn outside the frame of purposive, communicative rationality to out-do ourselves and be out-done' (Lash and Lury 2007: 207).

The revival of physical activity associated with digital culture can be read as indicative of a more sinister extension of commodity advertising, whereby it reaches into areas of subjective life previously withheld from contact with markets and commercial manipulation, but it also constitutes a new, more productive, even creative kind of cultural consumption. The virtual commodity is an 'integument, skin, interface, but also a deeper, generative, constructive and creative structure: a compressed structure' (2007: 196). In requiring us to play, it touches on the source of human creativity and inventiveness. In this sense, virtual commodities including computer games are profoundly ambivalent because, when we incorporate them into our lives, we also import the possibility of new kinds of dependency. Viewed in this way, the positive work of games and gamers in fashioning new social spaces becomes more of a source of concern because, rather than being spaces of deliberation and choice compatible with the democratic ideal of citizenship, the new spaces they open up in our experience may actually be openings to more profound kinds of manipulation and social control. The context for this is the economic changes associated with the rise of computer networks and their use to restructure the global economy. The changed role for individuals, the majority of whom have to work in this new environment, is a key factor in understanding the positive developments just described and essential to understanding their fundamental ambivalence.

2. The Gamer as a 'Streamlined Self'

If gaming has always involved a certain impetus towards the social and to creativity, the way this has worked out over the past four decades cannot be studied independently of the wider social context. Of particular importance here is the changed nature of economic activity in the digital or networked society and the implications of these changes for individuals. If human beings now find that their capacity to imagine and create shared spaces of social interaction is more dependent than ever upon commodities, this reflects the fact that they face a more arduous struggle than before to sustain a coherent sense of self. In face of the onslaught of changes to work and other aspects of social life wrought by the networked society, play becomes both a source of strength for people and another way in which their struggle to achieve personal autonomy, or even just a sense of coherence over the life course, is confronted by various kinds of domination and exploitation. The dynamics of the latter are explored more fully in connection with the games industry in chapter 4. Here, we will concentrate on the idea of the gamer as a 'streamlined self' – one who is thoroughly adapted to the new reality – before highlighting the possibilities that exist specifically in connection with gaming for positive interventions that might constrain some of the excesses of the new forms of power operative in contemporary society.

A number of social theorists have argued that the society based on computer networks produces new difficulties for people, especially in connection with the struggle we all face to maintain a coherent sense of self as a singular, meaningful project that perdures through time. The underlying sociological issue here is the rise of precarious and insecure forms of work. Richard Sennett (2006), for example, describes studies that asked university graduates in the 1960s and 1990s about the expectations they had of life beyond graduation. The earlier cohort had a much stronger sense of their lives as making sense as a kind of whole. They mapped that expectation onto ideas about fixed careers, enduring relationships and family lives. Each component of this picture had changed for the 1990s cohort, who were living through the transition to what Boltanski and Chiapello (2005) call the 'new spirit of capitalism'. Their expectations involved a succession of projects of variable duration, perhaps involving different skill sets acquired through successive periods of re-training. They did not anticipate lives as coherent totalities with a single overarching meaning, but rather saw the future in terms of disjointed segments with no connecting theme or sense of personal progression.

This kind of disrupted self-picture corresponds to what some see as a fragmentation of the self relative to the experience of subjectivity in earlier societies, induced by objective social changes (Adams 2007). Boltanski and Chiapello describe how the convergence of new technology and neo-liberal economic principles results in greater insecurity[5] for individual employees, with short-term contracts and temporary employment becoming the norm in many areas of work. Under these conditions, people lose the future as a reference point for contemporary meaning-making (2005: 421): there is no point in thinking about what I am doing today in terms of its ultimate significance for my career as a whole; instead I am obliged to focus on the project at hand and to make it as meaningful as possible in itself. In this situation of radically foreshortened temporal horizons, it becomes more difficult to assess situations, other people and the rightness of any given course of action. There is, they write, 'a kind of confusion about the meaning of everyday existence' (2005: 424).

This situation is not straightforwardly negative, however. One of its positive corollaries is that work itself has to be more interesting and it has to allow greater autonomy to individuals, mainly because the whole issue of motivation has been reconfigured. Networked organizations rely on people to manage themselves much more than the old hierarchical bureaucracies. For this to be successful, work has to be more appealing, less obviously coerced, and it has to involve people in a more engaging and even playful way than before. Life and work in the new society may be more insecure and less meaningful in the way that an old-fashioned career and family promised to be, but it is more of an *adventure*. The self who responds positively to this has, in a certain sense, no choice other than to do so. The option of being a miserable or sullen worker who works out of obligation to do so by a coercive management has been removed. Contemporary workers are scrutinized in much more individual and personalized ways than before. Exhibiting the correct outward attitude and, in particular, being open to establishing new connections with other workers are absolutely essential if you are to avoid exclusion and failure. In Barbara Ehrenreich's (2009) phrase, we have to 'smile or die' if we are to succeed in the networked society. The entire situation, then, is coloured as a kind of aesthetic performance. The ambivalence of this for the subject is neatly encapsulated in Boltanski and Chiapello's observation that we live in times that are 'subject to frequent, unforeseeable interruptions that are not only imposed, but supposed to be greeted with joy, as if discontinuity were the norm of a successful existence' (2005: 536).

Life in the new spirit involves a kind of cynicism (2005: 376) for individuals, who, on the one hand, probably do enjoy the playful and autonomous character of contemporary work more than a factory worker could ever have enjoyed his or her labour but, on the other, are now obliged to maintain a show of enjoying it all the time as well. In networked society we live a 'contradiction – between the exigency of adaptation and the demand for "authenticity" once connections have been created'. The resulting sense of having to simulate authentic relationships and attitudes, Boltanski and Chiapello write, 'creeps into the very core of the person' (2005: 460). This subjective condition is the context for the developments described in the previous section. As we will see in greater depth in chapter 5, cynicism runs through the new forms of sociality associated with on-line game play and other kinds of play that hold 'web 2.0' sociality together (cf. Lovink 2008).

The trajectory of games towards sociality is, however, real, for all that its results are compromised from the start.

The activity of playing computer games is in many ways consonant with the experience of work in the networked society. Carstens and Beck (2005), for example, argue that the 'gamer generation' have a distinctively competitive, even ruthless, attitude at work. Gamers, they write, 'will not learn for learning's sake alone' (2005: 24), confirming the idea that no work is undertaken in consideration of the long-term edification of the self. Computer games are very often competitive. They also involve play that is intense and repetitive to such an extent that even Jane McGonigal (2011), who argues that computer games offer a utopian alternative to reality, acknowledges that the activities we engage in with them often efface the conventional distinction between work and play. The paradigm case, historically, of a class of people for whom their work is a kind of play would be intellectuals and artists. Boltanski and Chiapello suggest that 'streamlined persons' in the networked society share a motivational psychology with those privileged (and sometimes not so privileged) groups. This infusion of the psychology of work with the ambience of play and sociability connects contemporary work with computer games and gaming culture.

In a situation where individuals do not progress through life but rather seek to do well in specific projects and to maintain networks that are functional in the present, people no longer hold on to any idea of personal progress. The rational course is to focus on playing the game well today. Playing well means maintaining popularity levels on Facebook, or establishing new connections on LinkedIn, while being no less intensely focused on the details of the project I am currently engaged with. It is permissible to enjoy the work but necessary to appear to be enjoying it and to share this feeling with other involved parties. That is the key to success in the game. What we see here is an aesthetic principle: maintenance of a desirable and attractive state of affairs in present time (healthy number of friends, happy-looking photograph, positive scores at work), displacing the notion of incremental development over the life course that used to underscore a sense of personal development or progress.

This context is not simply allegorized by computer games. Playing games and being interested in them is deeply isomorphic with contemporary forms of life, but gaming is more rooted than this implies in the ambivalence of contemporary work and of meaning-making processes related to the more fragmentary forms of selfhood that are salient today. What gaming allows people to do is sculpt a sense of self from resources that are familiar and which developed in tandem with the networked society, namely, computers and software. Playing games and playing them well involves the aesthetics of variable maintenance: performing learned actions with a precision and at times even grace that can generate patterns which can be enjoyed for their own sake. These activities fit with the new social order but they also compensate individuals for instabilities and insecurities experienced in the economic domain. Becoming good at a game and appraising the quality of one's performance in terms of a specialized language developed for the purpose lead to a sense of accomplishment reinforced by the recognition of one's peers.

It is natural, then, that gaming should possess an inherent appeal, since its mechanisms are, as we will see at greater length in chapter 3, those of a learned physiognomy, or *habitus*, that is in large measure consonant with a wide range of life practices in a time when we all spend too much time clicking in front of screens.[6] But it is equally obvious that gamers should seek validation and recognition for their activity. In the cultural space around gaming, players find recognition of their ability to dance the dance of variable management described above. Gaming requires manual dexterity, cognitive skill and familiarity with technologies and artefacts that are esteemed within the gaming community (to be good at *Halo*

(2001) is an achievement in the eyes of anyone who has played *Halo*). The sociological development of gaming and the emergence of a global gaming community are essential because it is through the development of gaming as an autonomous cultural practice with its own values that the ends of gaming (which are, clearly, trivial in themselves – they won't enable you to make anything of your life) are validated by being inscribed in the life of a collective (Boltanski and Chiapello 2005: 432). Part of the force that drives the development of gaming and its re-shaping of the social imaginary is this recuperative capacity it possesses in relation to the fragmented self.

What we see here, then, is an interplay between the social imaginary of the networked society, with its distinctive limitations, and the development of gaming as a practice partly in response to those limitations. As our sense of ourselves as participants in a meaningful social order comes under strain, we are drawn to practices which seem to offer some kind of compensation or recuperation from the process of fragmentation. Ironically, gaming practices are a key driver for the development of the very situation that produces that need for recuperation. At the same time, people are not drawn to games and play on the basis of a false consciousness: there are real benefits associated with play, for individuals and for society.

3. Social Theory and Critique

The history of this paradoxical situation lies in the assimilation of the 1960s counter-culture into contemporary management and business practices. Boltanski and Chiapello distinguish between a socio-economic critique of capitalism, which is historically associated with the labour movement and focused on issues of social security and remuneration for work, and what they call the artistic critique. The latter was associated with nineteenth-century bohemia, various kinds of dandyism and the ethos of artists and intellectuals. These groups are normally economically marginal but their critique of capitalism focused more on its hierarchical, bureaucratic and ordered character. The artistic critique of capitalism

> stresses the objective impulse of capitalism and bourgeois society to regiment and dominate human beings, and subject them to work that it prescribes for the purpose of profit, while hypocritically invoking morality. To this it counterposes the freedom of artists, their rejection of any contamination of aesthetics by ethics, their refusal of any form of subjection in time and space and, in its extreme forms, of any kind of work. (Boltanski and Chiapello 2005: 38)

In the revolutions that started on university campuses in Europe in 1968 and quickly spread to include workers, nearly toppling the French government in the process, the two kinds of critique came together. Workers and students opposed capitalism on two fronts, as unfair economically and as a restrictive and oppressive 'system'.

The convergence of the two kinds of critique is unusual in historical terms, and 1968 represents a kind of high-water mark for those who would like to see the overthrow of capitalism. However, in the years since, Boltanski and Chiapello argue, the artistic critique has been incorporated into the operation of the capitalist system. Networked capitalism is non-hierarchical and, as emphasized above, it allows workers to manage themselves at work. In place of stifling bureaucracies in which, to quote one mournful 68er, 'lives become careers', the new economy offers a succession of 'adventures'. This transformation of the work process entails a change in the individual who participates and is successful in it. The 'streamlined person' has to be adaptable, flexible and resilient to cope with the succession of changes they will encounter by always seeing in them opportunities and openings to extend their networks. Such a person resembles the artist intellectual much more than a traditional, suit-wearing business manager.

This transformation of work and of the individuals who have to do it represents an incorporation of the artistic critique, through which work itself has been aestheticized and made more like play. As I have pointed out in previous work (Kirkpatrick 2004), the aestheticization involved here extends to technology design and this is one of the contexts in which games are an important factor, a point to which I return in the next chapter.

Play was a key value for the 1960s counter-culture. The movement was strongly motivated by a desire to overturn the oppressive regime of bureaucratic, rationalized procedures and hierarchies that defined much of life in the 1950s and 1960s – the remainder being given over to a leisure filled with manipulation by the culture industry. For Richard Neville, editor of one of the counter-cultural magazines of the time and prominent spokesperson for the 'underground', the driving force of the counter-culture was 'playpower': a form of work that was 'done only for fun; as a pastime, obsession, hobby or art-form and thus is not work in the accepted sense' (Neville 1971: 213).

At the time it seemed as if such a vision of play as the naturally dominant force in human behaviour was incompatible with capitalism and the modern institution of work.[7] However, the changes described above, which have been made possible by the spread of digital technologies with 'friendly' interfaces, have undermined this idea. Boltanski and Chiapello refer to a 'displacement' within the capitalist system, whereby it responds to critique by incorporating it and evading it at the same time. No one could now decry contemporary work for its lack of a playful dimension. Instead, we are confronted with a resurgence of play (cf. Melucci 1996), but we find that it also has a surprisingly hard edge. As Boltanski and Chiapello put it, new ways of working

> demand greater commitment and rely on a more sophisticated ergonomics . . . [they] penetrate more deeply into

> people's inner selves – people are expected to 'give' them-
> selves to their work – and facilitate an instrumentalisation
> of human beings in their most specifically human dimen-
> sions. (2005: 98)

Incorporation of the playpower critique also occurred through the production of new kinds of commodity. These commodities mirror the transformation of work into play in so far as they represent an effacement of fundamental distinctions. From wholefoods and organic vegetables, through beauty and health products to mobile phones and other gadgets, the new range of commodities are strange because what they purport to sell is desirable mainly because it is authentic and therefore not a commodity in the traditional sense. As Robert Heilbroner puts it (in Boltanski and Chiapello 2005: 476), these commodities represent an 'expansion of capital within the interstices of social life'. Their paradoxical nature is related to a widespread and symptomatic anxiety about authenticity. We inhabit a strange situation in which everyone knows that there is no such thing as authenticity – the system can now sell us anything and everything, so there is no non-artificial outside – and yet authenticity continues to exert a spell-like hold over us, being both the key to what we desire in commodities and the enduring sign of a concern that all is not quite right with modern life. These paradoxes are, of course, the very stuff of computer games.

Dr Kawashima's Brain Train Program (2005) is exemplary for the new class of commodities and for many aspects of the transition from life in the old culture industry to the play of 'virtuals' that seems to define contemporary existence.

Dr Ryuta Kawashima is a real, human neuro-scientist who secured a degree of fame in Japan from a book[8] containing puzzles and exercises that he claimed would stimulate readers' brains and help them ward off degenerative processes associated with ageing, from normal changes in memory function to more serious impairments associated with senility.[9] In 2001 Kawashima was quoted in a British newspaper criticizing the games industry for producing games that were not good for people's brains.[10] His reward for these comments was that Nintendo approached him and challenged him to design a game that he considered healthy. So began the process whereby his books, with their puzzles and the associated narrative of brain fitness, became transmedial as they were converted into computer games played on Nintendo's hand-held device, the DS.

The game has three component parts. The first is a set of training programs that include exercises that involve memory, speed reading or information processing, and what are essentially times table tests or time-telling exercises, which involve simple reasoning. The second part is a set of related tests that are not for training but constitute a kind of assessment. When you have performed these you are assigned a 'brain age' by the cartoon Dr Kawashima. The effect of this can be disconcerting but also comical – new players are often alarmed (and amused) to find their brain is much older than they are. The third part of the game is the interaction with Dr Kawashima himself, the cartoon icon who addresses the player between tests offering words of reassurance, encouragement and advice. Appended to these core structures of the game is a set of Sudoku puzzles. Dr Kawashima claims that they may be useful brain training and helpful to you in your goal of achieving the optimal brain age, which is 20.

The game provides a simulated relationship with the character Dr Kawashima. As a player you have to manage your relationship with him, which entails regular visits to play the game by taking the exercises, running the tests and playing Sudoku. If you don't come for a few days he will greet you with, 'I didn't see you at all yesterday, it was sad', or 'It's been two weeks! Been busy have you? Ah yes, I understand'. If you leave it any longer, he gets sarcastic, asking 'who are you again?' If you just do the training, without running the risk of testing your brain age (the risk is that you might get an older brain age and this will result in unfavourable comparison with the other players on your machine), Dr Kawashima encourages you to take the test and measure your 'progress'. In addition to all of this, there are regular snippets of advice from the program to encourage behaviours and practices that are, or 'may be' good for your frontal cortex. For example, the doctor says, 'You brush your teeth when you wake up, right? I hope you do! While you brush your teeth try counting all the brush strokes. This will help to wake you up and warm up your brain!' In another intervention he tells us to control our bad habits: 'Your brain suffers when you lose conscious control of your actions. Trying to curb habits such as fidgeting or biting your nails is excellent training for your brain.'

In these moments, the game bears a marked similarity to the astrology column analysed by Adorno. Here, the player is cast as taking advice from a game, which is quite ridiculous, and, as with the earlier culture industry, many of the instructions concern the necessity of maintaining a positive outward appearance. The game also encourages us to acquire and sharpen skills that are particularly important to work in an informational society. Cognitive processing and analytical problem-solving, as well as flexibility in moving between scenarios, are all signs of a 'healthy brain'.

The game's central narrative construct, the brain age concept itself, is nearly as irrational as belief in astrology. Brain age claims some foundation in science, in that the game's exercises are based on a statistical correlation of performance in certain kinds of cognitive test with physical age. However, the issues in brain science are skilfully skirted around to ensure that even though the program and Kawashima himself actually fight fairly shy of making specific claims for its benefits,[11] we still have the feeling that we must be doing something like 'healthy exercise' when we engage in the memory tests and puzzle exercises.[12] The doctor's authority is preserved yet transported into territory where its legitimacy is unclear. The cultural impact of the game program

– *New Scientist* (2008) referred to brain training as a 'craze' – must be attributed to a prevailing, culturally specific anxiety about age and getting older – anxieties that can only be intensified in an age of endemic job insecurity and falling pension provision. The benefits of having an *older* brain are, of course, more difficult to test and to simulate. The game is presented as a kind of wrinkle cream for your brain and, like such creams, it appeals because we are anxious about getting old and losing our good looks or, in this case, our faculties.

Unlike the advice in the astrology columns, Dr Kawashima's does not concern social relationships and events but focuses instead on generic features, or permanent traits of the individual. As its guidance becomes more detached from specific times in this way, the game embeds itself more profoundly in the temporality of daily life. The verbal interventions described above show that, in a sense, the game is monitoring your activity and the messages constitute a kind of narrative opening through which the training exercises can find a place for themselves in your routine. At the same time, the exercises themselves are timeless, in the sense of being repetitive and unchanging. Once we achieve a certain brain age, the challenge is to maintain it by managing our performance in the various tests and, in so doing, to compete with other people, perhaps usually family members, who share access to the same DS.

The appeal of the brain age program is exemplary for Slavoj Žižek's (2009) observation that contemporary ideology has changed from 'symptomal mode' to being increasingly fetishistic. Žižek writes that in symptomal mode, 'the ideological lie which structures our perception of reality is threatened by symptoms *qua* "return of the repressed"' (2009: 65) and cultural practices were structured in response to this. Adorno's reading of astrology columns interpreted them in precisely this way, as sticking plaster advice addressed to a subject who is menaced by irrational urges from within, born of life in an excessively rational (determinate) social order. In contrast, the fetish, Žižek says, 'is the embodiment of the lie which enables us to sustain the unbearable truth' (2009: 65). The fetishist does not repress difficult truths but faces them, all the while clinging to an object that embodies the opposite belief. People who train their brains know that the activity cannot save them from the loss of their faculties, but they cling to the present and the (youthful) practice of playing the game, including trying to beat younger relatives, all the more intently.[13]

The temporality of the game positions it in an interesting way in relation to the goal of social critique. Objects of the old culture industry, from cars to clothes to hairstyles, were usually marketed on TV adverts and billboards several months in advance of their being available to buy. The temporality of the culture industry was one of endless deferral and its ideology was a regularly broken promise that fulfilment would come through the next purchase. Readers of the astrology column knew that their advice probably did not come from the stars, but the guidance kept them focused on pursuing the best pragmatic course to shape a positive future. In today's more fetishistic ideological context, we are too knowing to fall for anything like that, yet still seem to be focused on our symptomatic illusions. What mediates the desirable thing and its destruction in consumption now is not false ideological expectations but play. This gives play a peculiar function, perhaps with some critical potential. As Lash and Lury point out, the salient narratives associated with contemporary media objects stabilize and contain consumer activity, while play challenges their hold over subjects and their perceptions (2007: 108–9).

Play with a computer game can be contained by the game, in which case it is normally quite focused activity yet also repetitious, perhaps involving feelings of frustration as well as engagement for the player. Such play involves wearing away the illusion of the game as its characters and storyline collapse into routines that have to be mastered, but the activity is fundamentally joyless and normally holds no particular meaning for the player. But games can also make us laugh, as when we discover that our brain is very old, or 'prove' that it is really younger than our children's. Such disruptions are a way in which play shatters the hold of the game narrative. These events can put us in touch with other people, as our children might spend the next day trying to beat us, for example. What implications do these activities have for social critique?

According to Boltanski, there are three points at which an emancipatory sociology may win a foothold in contemporary society and culture. First, he suggests that philosophical anthropology discloses features of the human animal that can be referred to when we want to suggest that contemporary power goes too far in the development of synthetic realities. Play seems to me a strong candidate for such a starting point. As we will see in the next chapter, play is both a cultural universal and an essential moment in human creativity which has moved to the centre of contemporary social practice. It is unthinkable that play should be completely subordinated to the needs of the economic system or reduced to its function in a system of domination. The ambivalence of the computer game commodity and the culture in which it plays such a central role turns on this point. Boltanski suggests that people apply 'reality tests', more or less rigorously, to assess what is most firm and definite in their situations. In this context, normalizing discourses re-enforce the dominant conception of what is, limiting the capacities of the radical imaginary. But this 'reality' can be more or less fragile and the default position for human agents is uncertainty. The salience of experiences that familiarize us with the idea that things are never what they seem should be viewed in this context. Games are not straightforwardly complicit in contemporary ideology simply because of the disruptive and corrosive potential of play.

There is a second sense in which play may take on this kind of critical function in relation to the real. Play is integral to the human condition and, as I will discuss further in the next chapter, it is esteemed and evaluated in all human cultures, even if the terms of those evaluations vary. We may reasonably expect that corruptions of play, or just poor play, will be refused by players and this moment of refusal is perhaps another opening for serious kinds of reflection and connection with others. Here, play connects with Boltanski's second suggestion, which is that contemporary critique may identify what he calls 'immanent contradictions' in contemporary culture, which can be worked on. Computer games need players who appraise and criticize the games and they need a community that shares these ideas. The power of these new values lies in their capacity to break individuals free from one reality and connect them to an imagined community that opens out onto and shares another (Boltanski 2011: 42). As we will see in chapter 3, players have forged their own vocabularies for evaluating and criticizing games and generated a new community (of 'gamers') in the process. Emancipatory sociology may find an opening here, especially in the demands gamers can make for new and better games.

Finally, Boltanski suggests that social conflicts themselves offer resources for critique in so far as they thematize matters of real concern and thus create openings for critical sociological discourse. The existence of a gaming culture is a potential source of challenge to dominant forces in the gaming industry.[14] As Nieborg and Hermes (2008) point out, the corporations who make and sell games have a vested interest in controlling how games are appraised and 'the anticipatory function of the dominant industry discourse . . . focuses on technical, and thus economic, progress' (Nieborg and Hermes 2008: 140–1), to the exclusion of other aspects of gaming. Gamer demands may not be revolutionary, or even political in any conventional sense, but they are, in varying measure, independent from the control of game corporations and can take on an oppositional function. Here it is significant that games are caught up in contemporary conflicts over proprietorial claims of global corporations concerning the labour and products of gamers. From game 'mods' and cheat codes to various kinds of 'counter-gaming' (Galloway 2006), there are numerous signs within gaming as a technical and cultural practice of widespread dissatisfaction with this and, as Dyer-Witheford and de Peuter (2009) point out, these struggles extend to the production side of the industry too, where predominantly young workers in particular experience unpleasant working conditions as part of their 'adventure'. Here too there is no question of extrapolating a politics of wider application, but the relevant struggles are indicative of the form of contemporary social antagonism, especially the way that they involve a distinctive sensibility, which I characterize as cynical.[15]

CHAPTER TWO

Lineages of the Computer Game

The computer game has no single point of origin; no one person invented it and no single cultural context can claim to have shaped it. As Erkki Huhtamo puts it, 'electronic gaming cannot be traced back to any single source. It emerges from a slowly evolving, complex web of manifold cultural threads and nodes' (2005: 16). The aim of this chapter is to highlight the most important of those threads and to trace some of their entanglements, in order to get a better look at the knot of social, cultural and technical factors that formed the context of gaming. Looking at gaming's pre-history – the time when there were games for computers rather than computer games – enables us to see its entwinement in a revival of play and games; a transformation of the technological capacities of computing, and the artistic critique of capitalism mentioned in the last chapter. Each of these represents a significant historical and cultural trajectory in its own right. The computer game emerges where they intersect and it reacts back on each of them, contributing in important ways to the shaping of contemporary forms of play, the development of modern computing, and the reorganization of global economic and social practices. Historical investigation shows that each of the territorial centres in which gaming originates (Japan, the US and the UK) takes the lead at different points in the development of these themes.

This chapter begins by looking at how play and gaming were relegated to a subordinate role in modern culture in the time prior to digital games. The first section highlights the importance of play in human civilization, emphasizing its historical role as perhaps the fundamental source of human creativity and innovation. The discussion also addresses the issue of what constitutes a game and, consistent with the sociological approach outlined in the last chapter, argues that gameness must be understood as a mixture of quasi-anthropological constants with social and historical variations. This enables us to understand why play subsists in a culture that fundamentally disapproves of it. Adult play has been viewed, in the West at least, with suspicion for several centuries. Industrial society was concerned to contain the energies of play. Consequently, modern culture imposed an ordering dichotomy onto play and games according to which they were either strictly for children or inherently suspect practices often associated with the seamier side of life. This context sets the scene for computer games, whose first public manifestation is in 1970s entertainment arcades, adult pubs and clubs.

The second section elaborates on the social processes that have shaped the computer game, rejecting technological determinist accounts in favour of a measured social constructionism. Computers in the 1950s and 1960s were not thought about remotely as playful things. They were large machines, symbolically associated with the more serious aspects of government and corporate administration. In 1948, Howard Aiken of the US National Research Council said that America would likely only need five or six computers (Ceruzzi 2000: 13). They were big and expensive and only used for highly specialized activities. This section describes the 'dialectic of invention' (Chanan 1996) through which computer games were invented as cultural commodities by technology enthusiasts and entrepreneurs in the early 1970s. It highlights the important variations in the economic and cultural context of games through consideration of the different impact of the 1980s 'crash' on different geographic regions in which the new industry had established itself. This discussion emphasizes the importance of culturally shaped perceptions, as well as economic and management practices, in determining the resilience of gaming.

The computer game was an important factor in bringing about the cultural shifts that have changed the way that we imagine computers today, contributing to the development of design principles that made computers into friendly, even convivial, tools. In the final section, this chapter places the coming together of a cultural revival of play and computer technology into social and historical context. Exploring the central role of the 1960s counter-culture in the development of personal computing connects the early history of the computer game to the artistic critique of capitalism and the 1960s counter-culture discussed in the previous chapter. The computer game is a key part of the historical moment in which that movement was absorbed by capitalism and it has served as a vital conduit through which the artistic critique produces many of its effects.

1. The Revival of Play

Play defines most of what people do with computer games and this distinguishes them from other popular entertainment media, like films or books. Watching TV, for example, can have a playful element but when we engage computer games that element is central. As ludologists have argued (Wardrip-Fruin and Harrigan 2004), this has more profound implications than are commonly understood by scholars who approach games using established frameworks like those of media studies or sociology. Play is important and one way we know this is that it is both very old *and* subject to a great degree of cultural and historical variation. Play is something that all humans do and it has been present in all cultures. At the same time, it varies between contexts in its frequency, the significance that is invested in it, and the extent to which it is organized.

There is a problem here with definitions. Definitions of gameness in terms of competitions and prizes, for example, are accused of complicity in a masculine, capitalist social ordering of the play principle, which is present in many contemporary games but which might be overturned in some future social arrangement. As we saw in the last chapter, a key part of the work of critical theory lies precisely in unmasking false appearances and revealing the contingencies that underscore seemingly incorrigible institutions and practices.

However, the danger with pursuing such an approach too fervently is that it relativizes our idea of a game entirely to social contexts and conventions. This leads to an inability to say anything definite about what constitutes a game that might hold regardless of all situations, times and conventions. We need to understand games pragmatically, as prone to change depending on the cultural circumstances, but also as a deeply rooted feature of the human condition. There is a sense in which the human attraction to games transcends local historical contingencies and this also needs to be factored into our understanding. I propose, therefore, that we accept a definition that acknowledges the cultural universality of games while remaining sufficiently flexible to accommodate their diverse nature, function and significance in different social contexts.

Fortunately, a definition with sufficient nuance has been provided by the philosopher Bernard Suits:

> To play a game is to attempt to achieve a specific state of affairs [prelusory goal], using only means permitted by rules [lusory means], where the rules prohibit use of more efficient in favour of less efficient means [constitutive rules], and where the rules are accepted just because they make possible such activity [lusory attitude]. I also offer the following simpler and, so to speak, more portable version of the above: playing a game is the voluntary attempt to overcome unnecessary obstacles. (Suits 1978: 41)

Viewed in this way, gameness rests upon an anthropologically given disposition to play, which is a reliable constant of the human condition.[1] In every human culture people choose to create situations in which they impose constraints on themselves and their ability to achieve an objective, usually something trivial in itself, and they are guided in this by feelings associated with play. Caution is needed here to ensure the definition does not overload the ideas of play and a ludic orientation with too much content. The definition identifies a formal location or space that might be found doing all kinds of work in different cultural and historical settings. Play and games are always part of the magma, so to speak, that conditions cultural and social life, but the character they take and the purposes they serve are not determined independently of the institution of society.[2] Something is a game if and only if it combines play and the ludic attitude in some kind of enduring structure of rules and practices. It may also have other features (like a screen and a controller, for example) but the test of gameness is subtraction: strip away the other features and you still have a game, but remove the element of a freely chosen challenge that is specified in terms of unnecessary rules and whatever your object is, it is no longer a game. This is the reason why *Second Life* is not a game.[3]

Accepting this definition does not mean rendering oneself oblivious to important changes in the nature of the games played historically or the kinds of significance they can take on in different contexts. In fact, studying computer games involves recognizing that they have fashioned a new role for play in contemporary culture and that they are themselves shaped by the current position of play and games in that culture. Pierre Bourdieu (1995) made a similar point about art and works of art criticism. Like artworks, games respond to one state of the field (of knowledge and practice) in which they operate but this changes when they enter that field. They then operate in a new, redefined field and take on altered significance. This reflexive logic applies to computer games seen within the history of play and gaming.

According to Laura Kendrick, in Old English the noun *plega* and its forms were used to translate the Latin *ludus*, while *gamen* translated *jocus*. This is a reversal of what we might expect. Kendrick writes that '*Plega* and the verb *plegan* express physical activity involving quickness: hopping, jumping, fighting, dancing and even hand clapping (applause)' (Kendrick 2009: 48). The word 'play', then, is philologically subordinate to the word 'game' and inherited much of its modern sense from the first term. 'Game' signified fun, joy and ebullience before it came, in the fourteenth century, to signify something more static. As the verb *gamen* died out, the noun 'game' remained, retaining connotations of pleasure and levity, but now signifying something to be played (Kendrick 2009: 51): 'by the end of the middle ages, *pleie* had absorbed *gamen*'s original sense of the spontaneous bubbling up of joy, while the sense of *game* had become more formal, rule and strategy oriented' (Kendrick 2009: 53) Kendrick refers to a conscious effort on the part of medieval authorities to come up with strategies for the containment and redirection of play, through the imposition of rules that would 'turn it to a more profitable end' (2009: 54).

Play is a cultural universal, then, but it also has a history. According to Johann Huizinga, play is the primary source of human creativity and a 'play factor . . . produces many of the fundamental forms of social life' (1950: 173). As such, play underscores civilization but it is also a source of potentially subversive energies that can de-stabilize current arrangements of power. Its containment and the channelling of those energies is an important social function. The disciplinary societies of industrial modernity corralled play into a narrow association with children on one side and various kinds of competitive games on the other. The world that computer games entered was notably inhospitable to play and games, especially for adults. This led Huizinga to contrast play's productive and important role in human history with its degraded status in modern culture. He described modernity as, 'a rank layer of ideas, systems of thought and knowledge, doctrines, rules and regulations, moralities and conventions which have all lost touch with play' (Huizinga 1950: 75). Nonetheless, he argued, since culture 'is played from the very beginning', even though the play element may recede into the background, it is always there and 'at any moment, even in a highly developed civilization, the play-"instinct" may reassert itself in full force, drowning the individual and the mass in the intoxication of an immense game' (1950: 47).

Modernity's suppression of the meaningfulness of play can be seen particularly clearly in Japan because of the rapid, willed modernization of Japanese culture in the period after the Second World War. Andrew Feenberg (1995) describes how in the post-war period Japan consciously chose a modernization strategy that had implications for its ancient gaming culture. The game 'Go', he argues, has a competitive dynamic that was surrounded and contained by etiquette, protocol and rules of respect that hold between players of a certain standing. Games between 'Go' masters were public events that might last weeks, and journalists would write daily accounts of the game's drama for their readers. Players were cloistered each night, with the last move of the day recorded in a sealed envelope, to ensure that no player gained the advantage of a night's reflection prior to the next game-altering move. Modernization impacted on these rituals, moving them aside and relocating 'Go' in a more familiar, modern set of values associated with gaming, foregrounding the desire to compete and allowing players to play to win. Yasanuri Kawabata's (1972) *The Master of Go* describes how a young master shrugged off the constraints associated with respect for an older player and played for victory instead. Feenberg reads this as an incursion of the modern, which tends to strip down the intrinsic values of an aesthetic practice and, in this case, reduce games to mere contests. Here we can see in microcosm the fate of play and games in capitalist modernity during the time of the culture industry discussed in the last chapter, namely, that its intrinsic merits, especially its capacities to create and support values and meanings of wider interest, are diminished.

In contemporary culture play is still often unthinkingly[4] associated with children and with toys, but as Roberto Farne (2005) has shown, the association of play with childhood was only established in the late eighteenth century (Farne 2005: 170). From the mid-eighteenth century, a burgeoning symbolic association of play with children had been manifest in new kinds of objects. Children's books were published and toys were manufactured in Europe for the first time. According to historian Barbara Stafford (1994), Europe at this time 'was in the throes of changing from an oral, visual and aristocratic culture to a market-centred, democratic, print culture. Supposedly ignorant listeners and gullible onlookers had to be molded into silent and solitary readers' (1994: 1) In this context there was extensive debate over whether and how the 'lower senses' could be used in education, and this included the idea of play (Stafford 1994: 73–4) and the attempt to distinguish 'good', edifying games from bad ones (1994: 88). This distinction hardens in the course of the Industrial Revolution. Artin Göncü and Anthony Perone (2005) show how play was progressively downgraded as a cultural element in the course of the nineteenth century. 'Since the industrial revolution', they write, 'the Western world has considered leisure and labour as separate categories of activities' (2005: 138) and, 'in schools conceived as factories, play was acceptable only if it led to some utilitarian goals' (2005: 138). In the modern understanding, 'childhood was conceptualized as playful and exploratory whereas adulthood was conceptualized as logical and productive . . . a void in the literature about adult play', was accompanied by the 'trivialization of play even during childhood' (2005: 139; Farne 2005: 174–5).

Nonetheless, the nineteenth century was a time of fascination with visual entertainment technologies. People visited fairgrounds to look into stereoscopes and other gadgets, while they bought phenakistoscopes and zoetropes for their children to play with at home. The overriding perceptual paradigm of the age was one of stationary viewing (Kirby 1997). Exemplary here were the panoramas: great cylindrical buildings with vast paintings (or photographs in the case of cineoramas) on the interior surface, which were seen from a viewing platform at the centre of the device (Comment 2002). Here the human viewer is completely surrounded by the device that produces the spectacle. Only the eye is active as the body is captured and restrained. Jonathan Crary (1993) argues that the pleasure taken in these devices was overwhelmingly centred on a particular kind of play with the visual sense: the quality of the representations was less important than the experience of seeing itself. This is particularly evident in the case of the kaleidoscope and trumpeted in the phenakistoscope (the name means, 'deceptive view'). In fact, often the pleasure of these devices was in co-creating a visual phenomenon known to be unrepresentative of anything else (Crary 1993: 112).

By 1900 fairground spectaculars and displays had become articulated to commerce and selling: 'the sensual pleasures of consumption clearly triumphed over the abstract intellectual enjoyment of contemplating the progress of knowledge' (Williams 1991: 199). Older concerns resurfaced as critics discerned the emergence of developed arts of deception and manipulation in the use of spectacle to stimulate desire and consumption. The new department stores of the 1850s were 'places where consumers are an audience to be entertained by commodities, where selling is mingled with amusement' (Williams 1991: 204). Middle-class anxieties about the misuse of play and the manipulativeness and shallowness of entertainment, as distinct from real art and authentic culture, begin to dovetail with the Marxist critique of consumerism from this time. If play persists in modern culture, including adult play, it does so under a shadow of disapproval and suspicion, becoming increasingly marginal.

As Erkki Huhtamo has shown, slot machines and arcade machines are an integral part of the lineage of computer games, providing forms of 'amusement and gameplay' (2005: 3) that are highly resonant with the new form and in a cultural location, the arcade, that has remained constant. In Japan, the US and Europe, arcade gaming became popular in the 1880s and 1890s. In Europe and the US the machines were often banned because of their association with gambling. Nic Costa (1988) highlights various ruses machine manufacturers employed to get around the restrictive laws. These involved either emphasizing the role of skill over chance, or designing machines that offered straightforward transactions with a gaming sideline. Sometimes the transactions were not so straightforward. Machines were designed, for example, that gave players electrical shocks with alleged health benefits. In this way, the machine could be presented to the authorities as a vendor device selling shocks, with a gaming element that was incidental to the main transaction. Costa points out, 'in retrospect it is evident that the automatic gambling machine spent over half its production life posing as something else' (Costa 1988: 50), an observation that also resonates with computer games, for reasons to be explored later.

It is striking how similar many of these machines were, in terms of their manifest themes, to contemporary computer games. Gambling games often featured animated figures, for example. Since gambling was prohibited, players would be invited to 'compete' with the puppet or cut-out character (Costa 1988: 137). There were numerous football games, in which players controlled opposing players and teams: 'By the early 1900s the range of two player sporting games had widened considerably to include: tugs of war, cycle racers, rowing boats, boxers, table tennis players (the game of Ping

Pong enjoyed an enormous vogue at this time), and even swimmers racing in a tank of water' (Costa 1988: 139). From 1902 there were driving games; the 1920s saw games about spearing dragons; a game about shooting cats appeared in 1931 and a game called 'Smash Hitler' in 1939[5] (Costa 1988: 139, 149, 176). Many of these games featured controllers that involved much more varied and vigorous bodily action on the part of players than the repetitious cranking of a handle or switching between cards mentioned earlier. Costa describes a game from 1895 that involved players guiding avatars up poles using a system of cranks, for example (Costa 1988: 137). Gambling and slot machines became fully legal in the period after the Second World War, with German machines pre-eminent, mainly because the post-war government legalized gambling in 1953. In Japan, where Nintendo had been making various kinds of mechanical toys and cards since 1889, there was a slightly different arcade culture, centred on pachinko machines. Sega Incorporated entered this market in 1957. By the mid-1970s, 20 Japanese firms were active in producing arcade machines (Aoyama and Izushi 2003: 426).

The first computer game to be presented to the public, *Computer Space*, was placed in an arcade in 1971 by entrepreneur Nolan Bushnell. The fact that this was the first attempt to present computer games to a public outside of the narrow technical communities where people played with computers (of which more below) reflects the cultural space in which the new medium had to operate. Although *Computer Space* itself was unsuccessful, it nevertheless established a cultural template, so that for several years computer or video games were things you played in arcades and arcade games defined the gaming industry, especially in Europe and Japan. Arcade gaming boomed in the late 1970s. When games began to be made for home gaming platforms – the first was the Magnavox Odyssey in 1972 – they were invariably based on familiar arcade games like *Pong* (1972), *Space Invaders* (1978) and especially *Pac-Man* (1980). If it is true that computer games are an offshoot of the military-industrial complex (Dyer Witheford and de Peuter 2009), they have an equally essential lineage in the world of bars and clubs, which were the traditional home of pinball tables, fruit machines and pool tables. Indeed, the first arcade machines were manufactured in Japan by Taito, the company that made pachinko machines for Japanese arcades (Poole 2000: 168) and who made *Space Invaders* machines from 1978.

Arcade games promoted the idea that it was acceptable for adults to play games on computers – they were located in adult environments. At the same time, those environments have long been viewed with a degree of suspicion by the mainstream media and respectable society, reflecting the fact that they are relatively uncontrolled spaces, where people from different groups and backgrounds might meet. Like early cinema, arcade gaming was a source of anxiety for some, and concern was expressed in the 1970s that people were becoming 'addicted' to the machines and even stealing to pay for their 'habit'. These responses show that the presence of a new cultural practice was causing waves in the wider culture. The first news media controversy about computer game violence was caused in 1976 by the *Death Race* arcade game (Kocurek 2012). In the course of the 1970s, however, play with computer games began to make its way out of the shady arcades and into other cultural locations, reflecting a gradual reassertion of the importance and validity of play.

2. Technology and the Dialectic of Invention

The first instances of play with computers programmed for the purpose, which we might call 'games played on computers' as against computer games, were in research institutes in the US. When William Higinbotham invented *Tennis for Two* in 1958, it was, or became, an exhibition piece for the military installation (Brookhaven National Laboratory) where he worked (Malliet and de Meyer 2005) – it was not viewed as art or even as a new kind of sport. It had already been passed through a kind of social lens, or been mediated, and fixed in a certain, marginal cultural location, as trivial. The game was never marketed commercially and seems to have passed largely unremarked upon at the time, only becoming significant later when people asked about the origins of computer gaming. Similarly, when Steve Russell programmed *Spacewar!* in 1962 for the PDP-1 computer at MIT, interest in the game was limited to the tiny subculture then forming around computers. *Spacewar!*, like *Adventure* a few years later (1975), was modded[6] and passed around within this community (Abbate 1999: 206; Dyer-Witheford and de Peuter 2009: 6). Even within this group, people felt the need to rationalize the activity of making and playing games with reference to more important cultural practices. Jennifer Johns reports that *Spacewar!* had a diagnostic function for the computer (Johns 2006), for example, and Steve Kent has it that *Space Invaders* was originally designed as an aptitude test for programmers (Kent 2001: 116). The presence of such rationalizing statements tells us that at this stage these artefacts could not be viewed straightforwardly as computer games, since this was not a recognized class of objects and play with them was not a legitimate practice. These perceptions had to be produced through cultural work, as we will see in greater detail in the next chapter.

The fact that these games were made in research centres funded by the US military has led some to impute a militaristic connotation to the activity of playing with them (Dyer-Witheford and de Peuter 2009; Crogan 2012). There is an obvious and ancient affinity between agonistic game genres and military conflict, evident in things like the design of chess pieces to resemble warring family dynasties. Games have often been used for military training purposes (Crabtree 2010; Paris 2000), even before computer simulations were used to model conflict scenarios in the Cold War (Turner 2006). However, as I indicated above, play and games are also resonant with, indeed productive for, a wide range of other cultural practices. Indeed, Christian Ulrik Andersen argues that *Spacewar!*'s origins in the US military actually points to an inherent 'human need to present an alternative to cybernetics and early computer systems that were almost entirely related to the cold war' (Andersen 2012: 1). Which kind of meaning predominates and informs game designs is a function of the context and, as I stated in the introduction to this chapter, more than one context has shaped the computer game. As one of the founders of modern computer science, Joseph Weizenbaum, put it, 'the computer is a playing field on which one can play out any game one can imagine' (in Roszack 1968: 7). It would be an error to read too much into the fact that the first games were programmed on military computers – this point of origin does not determine their significance for the culture as a whole.

Similarly, the growth and spread of games as a cultural form was not determined by the rise of computer technology but rather the two developments should be understood as interdependent. Malliet and de Meyer (2005) maintain that technological change runs 'like a red line' through the history of computer games, determining critical changes in the development of the form. They argue that, 'the continuous development of computer technology has served as the driving force behind the ever-increasing sophistication of video games' (2005: 24). According to this determinist view, the development of computer game features, like more sensitive controllers, or sharper graphics, or higher speed of on-screen action, is a function of the available technology that enables game designers to implement their pre-existing ideas about games more effectively, resulting in better and better games. The difficulty for this perspective is that it overloads our image of the past with ideas illegitimately imported from the present, assuming that the creators of the form knew in advance what a computer game was and what would make a good one. For example, the first motion-sensitive controller, 'le stick' (developed by Data Soft Inc. in 1984) can be seen as anticipating Nintendo's *Wii*-mote (2006), in that both fulfil the aspiration for fuller body involvement in control systems. This aspiration then seems always to have been present, just waiting for technical fulfilment and inscribed, as it were, in the technical trajectory of gaming.

Such a narrative overlooks the false starts, the failed ideas, the innovations that seemed like 'the future' at the time they were introduced but which came to nothing, perhaps even things that defined a good game for a while but are now forgotten. For example, the Nintendo 'Power glove' controller of 1989–90 (Scheff 1993: 230) aimed at including a wider range of manual movements into the control system, but it was not a great success and when we see one now it looks strange and anomalous. Similarly, numerous 1980s experiments with light pens as data input devices, or Atari's 1984 *Mindlink* controller, which purported to interpret players' thoughts,[7] are the kinds of failed idea that litter the history of games. The point is that they were every bit as significant to the people who created and used them as the devices that find an echo decades later. No linear technical history brought us from a state of ludic primitivism to the 'advanced condition' of the *Kinect* and the *Playstation* network. *Spacewar!* was experienced as a new phenomenon and not as the anticipation of something else. The study of how we acquired our current idea of what makes a good game is more messy and its variables more intertwined than technical determinism can account for. The dominant cultural perception of a computer game currently involves a screen, a controller with buttons, and certain kinds of action on either side of the screen. To count as a computer game is to be consistent with this perceptual template. But this template had to be produced and established in the culture; it was not technically determined. At issue here is the mesh of social and technical determinations in the computer game object.

My approach to this is a kind of pragmatic constructionism. For social constructionists, the shape and function of technology is an effect of the perceptions and descriptions of social agents, who project their desires onto an artefact or design and collectively determine what it is 'really' for (Bijker et al. 1989). Viewed in this way, computer games are the outcome of how a given community makes sense of its members' natural inclination to play with complex artefacts. The activity might be deemed trivial, or elevated into an esteemed cultural practice. Choices made by relevant social groups mediate the role of play in the culture, combining it with affordances of new technology to produce a new technological artefact, the significance of which cannot be separated from its social context.

However, it should be acknowledged that there is a certain arbitrariness to constructionism, which can make it seem as if our current designs are subject to no limiting influence deriving from the past or the real, physical world we inhabit. In fact, the range of what people seek in technology design is in practice constrained by the kinds of creature human beings are and the kinds of action they pursue in the world (Kirkpatrick 2008). These things are not straightforwardly a matter of human nature but they are, in Jürgen Habermas' (1987) phrase, 'quasi-transcendental' in the sense that they do not change much or often and we need to assume their presence if we are to make sense of much that we see going on in the social world. Taking this more pragmatic approach,[8] it seems that changes to available technology often present new affordances, which people take advantage of to make tools and expedite practices they might have engaged in anyway. This philosophical perspective throws the interest of computer games for social theory into some relief. Given that play is natural to humans and some other animals,[9] it makes sense to look at the development of computer games as arising out of an innate human disposition that has been drawn out and developed in conjunction with computers.

Understood in this way, technology design should be viewed as a kind of dialogue of human purposes with technical artefacts, sometimes involving the recalcitrance of matter and its occasionally senseless intrusions and constraints. Michael Chanan has observed something like this in the early history of cinema, which he describes in terms of a 'dialectic of invention'. Describing numerous dabblings and experiments with cinematic technology, Chanan writes that

> what we're dealing with here is a generative process which had neither a single starting point nor any clear idea where it was going. It is a mistake to go searching for a linear progression instead of registering the real movement of cause and effect, in which any one cause might have several effects and any effect might have several causes. (Chanan 1996: 111)

There is no pre-determined end or *telos* that controls the process of technology development. Technology cannot be said to objectively 'improve' because we have no single, fixed standard relative to which we could measure such progress.

This kind of dialectic – a to and fro of ideas ungoverned by any specific purpose or goal in interaction with burgeoning technology whose limits are not fully understood – can be seen at work in the design of computer games, especially in their formative period. Playful interaction with a computer leads to perhaps surprising effects, which are then retained in a subsequent, slightly different iteration. We can imagine this process as somewhat senseless and as pleasurable in itself and examples of such aimless dabbling can be found in the recollections of the first home computer users. Most computers of that era had no prescribed functions or pre-written software to tell people what to do with them. One of Steven Levy's (1984) respondents recalls the first home computer, the 1975 Altair 8800,[10] as having flashing lights but no clearly defined function, while Fred Turner (2006) describes how for early users part of the fun of the machine was finding out what, if anything, it could do.

In the course of the 1960s, the size of computers reduced as new storage media became available (Pfaffenberger 1988;

Ceruzzi 2000). Silicon chips meant that small machines could process information quickly on a scale that would formerly have required a machine big enough to fill a room (the PDP-1 was referred to as a 'hulking giant'; Levy 1984). This change, coupled with the presence of a small but growing group of people who liked computers and electronics for their own sake, gave rise to the notion that small computers might be used to make life better for ordinary individuals and communities. This idea, which originated in the 1960s counterculture, resulted in a series of experiments in the manufacture of home computers, starting with the Altair. These machines were carried to a wider public by games, which made them accessible and gave people a reason for taking an interest in them.

The first small computers, however, were demanding technical objects. It is reckoned that most Altairs, for example, which came as self-assembly kits, were never actually built because to make them work required technical knowledge well beyond those of the normal electronics enthusiast, who at that time enjoyed things like tinkering with radio sets and model railways. Games for the machines were central to the appropriation of the computer by the emerging subculture and to its growth as a social movement. Game programs were vital in introducing computers to people who otherwise encountered them as pointlessly difficult.[11] Between 1961 and 1972, *Spacewar!* was repeatedly hacked and copies of the game were exchanged within this group. The usefulness of games to promote computers was not completely unnoticed by commercial forces either. Turner describes how salesmen for Digital Equipment Corporation (DEC) started to use borrowed copies of *Spacewar!* to demonstrate their small computers to putative clients (Turner 2006: 134). Games were the most accessible programs for the machines of this time: it was easy for people to see that a computer could 'do something' if it played a game and it was relatively easy to become involved in the activity.

In the US in particular, the confluence of play and computer technology led, in the course of the 1970s, to mass production of dedicated home gaming machines. In 1972 the Magnavox Odyssey brought a version of the arcade game *Pong* to American living rooms.[12] It was followed by machines like Fairchild's *Channel F* (1976), the first system to use cartridges, and later the *Mattel Intellivision* (1979) and *Colecovision* (1982) machines. In Japan, Nintendo manufactured *Color TV Game 6*, a console with six versions of light tennis. As with the arcade games discussed above, here too the computer game had a kind of lineage: there were precedents in the form of other leisure entertainment technologies that had made their way into people's homes, especially radios (1930s) and televisions (1940s). As mentioned previously, in the century before broadcast media, people played with toys, gadgets and board games, and strategy games have been commercially produced since the late nineteenth century (Paris 2000: 140–2). The biggest-selling home gaming machine of this era was the Atari VCS, which was sold in the US from 1976 until the industry crash in 1983. According to Malliet and de Meyer (2005), the principal reason for its success was Atari's connection with the arcade industry, which meant they had ready access to an established library of games that were already well known to putative customers for the machine's cartridges.

These devices entered homes as playful adjuncts to the established array of domesticated entertainment technology, especially television.[13] It is significant that many of them only played one game because it tells us that the symbolic alignment of the machines positioned them as toys, as games on computers, or with a computerized element, rather than computer games in the contemporary sense. To some extent this changed at the end of 1976 with Atari's 2800 cartridge-based system, because this meant more games were available, but even then the symbolic association of home gaming with children's toys was definitive.

This became most apparent when the US games industry 'crashed' in 1982–3. Contemporaneous accounts of this episode give the impression that many people (parents in particular) had never expected computer games to last more than a couple of years anyway, and that perception may have contributed to making the US market, in particular, quite fragile. The differential impact of the crash on each of the three centres of gaming at this time is revealing with regard to the position of gaming as a cultural practice in the late 1970s and early 1980s.

In 1982 the industry that had become established producing game cartridges, mainly for the Atari machine, faced a catastrophic collapse in demand and by the middle of 1983 there was almost no games industry to speak of in the United States. A few explanations have been put forward for this. Montfort and Bogost (2009) point to the overproduction of unimaginative *Pac-Man* conversions. They also refer to the *ET: the extra-terrestrial* game, based on the movie, which was generally considered to have been a very poor product. Consumers felt that they were being sold rubbish and stopped buying game cartridges. Dmitri Williams refers to 'inept management' (n.d.: 4) by Atari, while Montfort and Bogost (2009) also refer to 'mismanagement' by the console firm. Nick Dyer-Witheford and Greig de Peuter express this in autonomist Marxist terms,[14] writing that Atari failed to come up with organizational and disciplinary forms to contain 'the playful genius of immaterial labour' (2009: 14) involved in making games. There is consensus that Atari did not even attempt control over the quality and quantity of games produced for their console.

Consequently, Malliet and de Meyer write of a crisis of overproduction of software (Malliet and de Meyer 2005: 34), especially ball and paddle games. However, they also report that the crash was attributed by many people at the time to the superiority of a new generation of small computers over the home entertainment platforms. This explanation is repeated by Deuze et al. who attribute what they call the 'early 80s implosion' to 'the move of games from arcades to the home' (2007: 336). On this analysis, people were switching loyalties to home computers because they could be used for playing (and making) games but also for other functions.[15] In keeping with most historians, Malliet and de Meyer reject this explanation, arguing that the two platforms 'simply developed along different routes rather than intersecting with each other' (Malliet and de Meyer 2005: 36). However, this contradicts other parts of their own analysis. On one hand, they maintain that console games were better for certain kinds of physically robust play, for example, but then have to acknowledge that such play was common in connection with important PC games as well (they mention *Monkey Island* (1990), which had 'quick rhythm with a good dose of comedy' (2005: 37)). They also note that games in the *Zelda* series, which have appeared on various Nintendo systems since 1986, have borrowed ideas from a succession of different PC genres.

It seems most likely that the contemporaneous explanation holds more strongly for some territories than for others. Specifically, the UK market for games held up in 1982–5 because there the home computer was already, before the US crash, the preferred platform for playing games. Dedicated console gaming systems had never caught on in Europe to the same extent as in the US, and they did not acquire the definitive association with gaming. Meanwhile, small computers, often imported from America but also manufactured in nearly all European countries, were popular. In the European marketplace the fact that computers could be sold as 'educational' to parents, while children knew that they were really for playing games, was always key (Selwyn 2010). In this sense, the argument that small computers were superior holds for the UK and explains the persistence of gaming there throughout the period of the US crash. In Japan, the crash impacted on Nintendo and other companies primarily as a loss of exports and a redefinition of the symbolic environment in which games and gaming devices were thought about. The notion that gaming was a fad that had ended[16] posed a problem of representation rather than of short-term demand for Nintendo, which, according to Scheff (1993), they negotiated by presenting their new Famicom console, when it appeared in 1983, as a home entertainment system that could also be used for business and home computing purposes. The crash, it seems, was experienced differently in each of the three main centres of gaming and different explanations may be needed for its consequences in each setting.

Most of the historical scholarship to date has exaggerated the uniform impact of the crash, largely as a result of generalizing from the American situation and of over-identifying the fate of the games industry with that of console and cartridge manufacturers. At the time, US developers were well aware that the industry was doing well outside the US. A British computer enthusiast magazine, *Commodore User*, published in 1985 in the wake of the crash, carried an article from Dan Gutman, the editor of an American gaming magazine that had gone out of business. He addresses his British readers in the following terms:

> I can see that you folks are still computer game *freaks*. It seems like there are hundreds of computer game companies over there, and they're cranking out thousands of titles. It's obviously your passion, your reason for existence.

He goes on to describe the rise and fall of the US industry, including the tragedy of his own magazine, attributing the demise of the US industry to the arrival of home computers – it is important to remember that his article is in *Commodore User* magazine, not, say, *Computer and Video Gaming*. Gutman concludes his piece:

> America is confused about computers and computer games right now. Most people agree that 'computers are the future', but they don't know what they would do with one if they had one. While computers have revolutionized the American

office, only 13% of American households own computers today. These days, the software bestsellers are music programs, art programs, diet programs, and home finance programs. And I'm sitting here . . . waiting for the next phenomenon. (*Commodore User* 20, May 1985, p. 68)

From the depths of its crash, then, the American industry eyed a UK gaming scene that continued to thrive. This discrepancy is salutary in reminding us that games and gaming as cultural practice do not originate in one national territory or a single cultural context.

In the United States, the relative lack of a hobbyist computing culture that might have continued gaming on small home computers can probably be, at least in part, attributed to the over-rapid commercialization and commodification of games in the late 1970s.[17] The DIY culture of hacking and modding games did not spread because games had already been successfully marketed as toys for children. Meanwhile, Japan's culture industries were, as Izushi and Aoyama (2006) point out, differently organized, being more porous in relation to each other and so well placed and resourced to respond to the presentation issue of 1982–3. In the early 1970s, Nintendo recruited artists and technologists and gave them remarkable latitude to experiment and come up with games – a policy they pursued as an alternative to merely importing games from the US (Scheff 1993: 22). At this time, Japan was seeing a strong new industry of anime films, associated with television more than cinema (Napier 2005), and experiencing its own 'play revival'. This made the Japanese industry well placed to respond to the shift in perceptions associated with the collapse of the US market. Meanwhile, the relative failure of the first console machines in the UK, as against the large sales of home computers, had the curious effect of making that country the locus of a vibrant 'cottage industry' in games production. As we will see in the next chapter, this was the context in which gaming established itself as a practice with intrinsic value and became the basis of an identity that turned out to have much sought-after recuperative powers in the next few decades. More than anything, the impact of the crash on the US gaming scene reflects the lack of cultural autonomy enjoyed by the practice at this time, which made it easy to dismiss games as a fad no better than its worst exemplars.

3. Artistic Critique and the Transformation of Computing

The dialectic of invention that shaped computers as we know them today involved a culture of play on one side and changes in the possibilities presented by computing technology on the other. The development of computer technology to the point where it is almost coterminous with the idea of society itself has been driven by this dialectic. In it we see the process of capitalism's absorption and evasion of the counter-cultural artistic critique in detail. It is at the point where that critique touches on and shapes technology that we can identify perhaps the most important consequences of that assimilation process This was anticipated by some critical theorists, some of whom were personally associated with the 1960s counter-culture.

The 1960s movement was predominantly critical of, and on occasion just opposed to, technology. Its motivational basis lay in disaffection with the forms of social organization associated with industrial society. People were suspicious of technology's role in the domination and exploitation associated with 'the system' or capitalism. Much counter-cultural writing emphasizes the role of industrial and computer technology in modern bureaucratic societies and seems to aim at a romantic return to nature. Theoretical sources important to the counter-culture targeted 'technocracy', an organizing principle found on both sides of the Iron Curtain, in which experts and technical systems held sway over important social decisions. Choices concerning the direction society should go in, its priorities for the future, would be made without reference to ideas and values mediated through democratic discussion.

Instead, technical imperatives would determine what had to be done, from reorganizing work processes to the siting of nuclear power plants. The role of human beings and of rational, deliberative processes seemed to be effaced in a culture that only esteemed the technical value of efficiency. The clearest exponents of this view were critical social theorists like Herbert Marcuse, who in May 1968 flew to Paris to address students involved in the uprising, many of whom had been inspired by his ideas (Feenberg and Freedman 2001).

Technology was clearly a big part of the imagined future that the students and young workers of 1968 did not want for themselves. They feared a life of repetitive drudgery under the command of austere machines programmed by others. They rejected the hierarchical organization of work that might place them in a management role where they imposed such a life on others. Above all, perhaps, they craved a life that would involve play, adventure and self-determination. The critique of technocracy was an important part of the 'artistic critique' of capitalism discussed in the previous chapter. While Marcuse himself was not 'anti-technology', he was critical of modern society's 'construction of techniques' that sought to dominate the natural world and to pacify human beings into lives of standardized, controlled consumption (Marcuse 1964). It is easy to see how this perspective might have comported with romantic 'back to nature' and 'small is beautiful' type arguments, which also circulated at this time.

However, the counter-culture also included a technophilic strain. In its American version in particular, sections of the movement were also drawn to gadgets and devices (Roszack 1968), including the new, small computers that began to appear for sale in the early 1970s. For some, playing around with computers was a source of aesthetic pleasure in itself, but it could also contribute to creating the infrastructure for a new kind of society, in which various kinds of domination associated with hierarchy and bureaucracy would no longer exist. In this vision of the future, computers might serve as 'tools for conviviality' (Illich 1971), connecting people and communities in networks that would be both productive and based on the free association of individuals.

In the US context, it was 'hippy hackers' who first developed the idea, at the time radical, of computers for everyone. As Freiberger and Swaine point out, it took several years for any of the established computer manufacturers to realize the potential of micro-computers as the kind of thing that ordinary people might want to own and use for themselves. The first computer that might fit under a desk, the PDP-8, was made by Digital Equipment Corporation in 1965 (Freiberger and Swaine 1984: 20), but there were no plans to market it outside of the scientific research community: 'Without exception, the existing computer companies passed up the chance to bring computers into the home and onto the desk . . . the microcomputer was created entirely by individual entrepreneurs working outside the established corporations' (Freiberger and Swaine 1984: 17–18). In the midst of 'women's lib', the hacker Ted Nelson wrote a book called 'computer lib', which was a manifesto for those elements of the counterculture who believed computers could change people's lives for the better. This strain of the counter-culture wanted to create a new kind of technology that could serve human beings and communities rather than controlling them.[18] Along with others who set up clubs to learn about computers and explore their capabilities, Nelson argued that computers could be emancipatory tools, the infrastructure of a revived community in control of its own destiny.

Fred Turner (2006) argues that this culture around small computers was not really influenced by the new left political movement, which was concerned primarily with economic and other injustices arising out of the capitalist economic system, but was more concerned with what we would now call 'lifestyle' issues. The hackers were playful experimenters and they sought to use computer technology as a mechanism that would make a more integrated and happy way of life possible.

The playfulness of the movement is evident in the names they chose for their organizations, which included: Golemics Inc.; Loving Grace Cybernetics; Itty Bitty Computer Company; Chicken Delight Computer Consultants, and Kentucky Fried Computers from North Carolina. These kinds of slightly zany names for businesses are perhaps commonplace now but, in the grey world of 1960s commerce, they stood out. As Freiberger and Swaine put it, the names of the clubs and early manufacturers of home computers signified an 'amorphous subculture of technofreaks, hobbyists and hackers, people untrained in business skills and more interested in exploring the potential of the microcomputer than in making money' (1984: 59).

Games were conspicuously central to the process whereby computers were converted from machines of big government and social control into tools of democracy and personal empowerment. As indicated above, between 1961 and 1972 *Spacewar!* was repeatedly hacked and modded between hobbyists and playing the game was many people's first experience of a computer. Fred Turner refers to an article by Stewart Brand which appeared in *Rolling Stone* magazine in 1972, 'Spacewar: fanatic life and symbolic death among computer bums'. In it, Brand described 'the countercultural force of *Spacewar*, of computers and of the freewheeling collaborative culture that surrounded them' (Turner 2006: 116), using the game to present computers as part of an alternative vision of society. Even Dyer-Witheford and de Peuter, who are generally keen to emphasize the military origins of the computer game, acknowledge that 'virtual play was an invention of, and ingredient in, the radical counter-culture of the sixties and seventies' (2009: 6).

Similarly, from 1975 the growth of networked computing was in large measure a function of people developing *Adventure*-type games. In the early 1970s the Advanced Projects Research Agency (ARPA) developed the network that became the Internet, the ARPANET. ARPA viewed their network primarily as a method of sharing resources. Its communicative potential, including e-mail for example, was not integral to the original design of the project (Abbate 1999: 106–7). However, students and others built these aspects on top of the core infrastructure and games were foremost among these applications. As Janet Abbate writes: 'network users created a whole new set of applications (for example the role-playing games known as "multi-user dungeons") to fulfill their desires for entertainment, social interaction, and self-expression' (1999: 200; cf. Hafner and Lyons 1996: 189). What really enthused people about using the new networks was games, especially *Adventure* (Abbate 1999: 206), which was a feature of the network even before e-mail. Similar patterns can be identified on other networks around the world.[19]

In these developments we see computer games playing a leading role in the qualitative transformation of modern technology. Games contribute to the idea of computing as something that everyone can do and which can be pleasurable, even life-enhancing. They also feed directly into the development of 'user-friendly' and easy-to-use interfaces, which transformed computers towards the end of the 1980s, reorganizing computing under metaphors like the 'desktop' and situating human–computer interaction in line with narrative orderings familiar to users from other, 'natural' contexts of action. Brenda Laurel (1995), Nicholas Negroponte (1995) and other pioneers of the friendly human interface all refer to games as the first software to develop these principles and apply them to interface design (Kirkpatrick 2004). These developments were identified by no less a figure than Timothy Leary, 1960s advocate of the consciousness-raising powers of LSD, as a continuation of his mission. 'Today's human interface designers', he wrote in 1989, are about to unleash 'undreamed of changes in the consciousness of people all over the world by giving them a tool for expanding the power of their minds'

(Leary 1990: 229). He envisaged designs that over the course of the coming decade would 'link amplified individual minds into a global groupmind' (Leary 1990: 230).

Viewed in this light, games have played a role in the progressive aestheticization of technology envisioned by critical theorists like Marcuse (1978) and Andrew Feenberg (2002). This transformation of technology adds a new dimension, however, to Boltanski and Chiapello's account of capitalism's 'adaptation' to the pressures for change that came from the 1960s counter-culture (the artistic critique). They identify the anti-technological orientation of the artistic critique, highlighting the dominant tendency within the counter-culture, which, as we have seen, was anti-technocratic and focused on technology's social control functions (2005: 440). In arguing that capitalism 'internalizes' this critique, however, they neglect to deal with the transformation of its technical infrastructure. The work process changes to become more playful and engaging, and it does so within a social context of less stability and more precariousness for employees. What makes this change to the work process possible, however, is the transformation of the computer itself. Machines with seductive (Turkle 1995) interfaces, running routines that present only moderate challenges to users, integrated within representations that have narrative coherence and perhaps even include positive aesthetic 'pay-offs', are all fundamental to contemporary, workplace technology design. The ludic origins of these design principles are well established.

Like most authors on informationalization and the networked economy, Boltanski and Chiapello tend to evaluate technology only in economic terms, that is, according to whether it contributes to improvements in economic performance. It is evident, however, that the aesthetic transformation of computer technology, in which games play a central role, confirms the central thrust of their argument and extends the reach of their critique. Technology design is always a contested, political process, although it is rarely recognized as such. Computer games have informed the design of post-industrial technology, powerfully contributing to its aestheticization. Here, as in other dimensions of society, however, the artistic critique's fulfilment of its aims has been bought at the price of an evasion on the part of the system and a series of displacements. In place of hard, brutal technology that could quite easily be criticized for its inhuman effects, we now have glossy, colourful tools that demand a different kind of engagement, to an extent modelled on play with a computer game. The aestheticization of contemporary technology is powerfully suffused by the idea of play and, as we saw in chapter 1, this is allied to the new emphasis placed on individual creativity and flexibility in the 'new spirit of capitalism'. Power is then displaced away from management at the hard point of production to self-management through the intense, playful labour of scrutinizing and controlling variables pertaining to one's own performance. Work and life are a game, with all the ambiguity that term brings to any situation.

Computer games are the outcome of a revival of play in connection with a new technology. But the collision of these forces has happened under specific historical and cultural conditions. As I indicated in the previous chapter, computer games are a kind of eruption of play and technology within the old culture industry. Games have been technically constant over most of human history, drawing on available materials and only occasionally importing new methods or means from the technological context. With computer games this is completely altered. The power of technology and its symbolic association with the new, even with the future itself (Roe Smith and Marx 1994), informs a massive expansion of play and games that has been a principal driver in the emergence of new spaces over the past three decades – the spaces of a new social imaginary. Computer games are charged with the force of technology, so that as well as being appealing toys, they also carry symbolic connotations of dynamism and progress. On the other hand, digital technology in various (perhaps most) of its contexts became associated with play. There is a reflexive interaction here of social practices and technology designs that forms an essential part of any understanding of the sociological importance of computer games.

Here we should notice an important difference between computer games and traditional games, which concerns a reflexive consequence of this intersection of play with technology. Because computer games are technological objects, they inherit some of our expectations of technology. In particular, we expect it to be dynamic, to be a site of constant innovation, perhaps even to drive wider changes. These expectations do not apply to older games: attempts to change the rules of games like football or chess are generally viewed with suspicion by lovers of the games. The situation is very different with computer games. Each game is expected to offer some new enhancement to the playing experience, as well as just being a good game. Our expectations here are constitutive: game designers know that to an extent their products will be appraised for their novelty and innovation. Part of what it means to make a good computer game is to be experimental. In contrast, Lionel Messi is expected to produce excellent passes every time he plays football, but no one expects him to invent new ways of kicking the ball. Johan Cruyff did this, of course, and is immortalized in consequence. For computer game designers, innovation of this kind is part of what is most esteemed in their craft, although it is something that is increasingly difficult for them to achieve, for reasons discussed in chapter 4.

Historically, there have been several such moments of innovation and the prevailing idea of what counts as a computer game – the kinds of action and effect we expect to find when we encounter one – has changed. In this way, our idea of what a game is and the reality of what games are and of what makes a good game have been altered. Each gaming innovation has modified the field of perception that defines games for us, in accordance with the reflexive logic described at the end of the last chapter. In all likelihood, this kind of change will occur again in the future because it seems to be part of what defines computer games. The next chapter positions this expectation in the culture that was formed around computer games in part through the agency of gaming magazines like *Commodore User*.

This chapter has looked at the multiple points of origin of the computer game, while refusing the idea of a moment of inception, or a single point at which computer games were invented. It stressed instead that computer games emerged at the thick points of intersection of developments in more than one field of cultural practice. Although the first recognizable computer games were developed in a US military context, the new form was not determined in its development exclusively by technical imperatives or by values drawn only from that sphere. Multiple social and cultural contexts have shaped the form, including counter-cultural values and the kinds of play and games that were prevalent in the period immediately before computer gaming. Indeed, our prevailing idea of what technology is has been altered by the presence of computer games and their influence on interface design. As the computer game has taken shape, so it has participated in the construction of our current social reality, and understanding what the computer game is requires that we grasp it as both consequence and cause of significant cultural changes that have occurred over the last 40 years. Reflexive modifications of games and gameness have reverberated through our culture and society, affecting our perceptions of work and technology as well as having consequences for what counts as a good way to live. As games have come to occupy a place in the culture where they amount to much more than just a fad, so they have been associated with new perceptions, practices and values, all integral to life in the new capitalism.

CHAPTER THREE

The Formation of Gaming Culture

As indicated in the previous chapter, the crash of the early 1980s played out in different ways in each of the main centres of computer gaming. In most historical accounts, the period 1983–5 is defined by the seeming disappearance of games, prior to Nintendo's revival of the industry in 1986. However, this narrative betrays a significant bias towards the dedicated games console as the privileged platform in the evolution of computer games and, as indicated in the previous chapter, it is also somewhat US-centric. One effect of these distortions has been to obscure cultural developments in the early 1980s that were fundamental to the success of computer games in the years after 1985. It was during these years that gaming began to secure a kind of cultural autonomy that it did not have while it was perceived merely as a fad or a popular craze. Through the establishment of game-specific evaluative norms and criteria, which occurred primarily through the medium of computer and gaming magazines produced outside the US, gaming became something more than this. It was precisely during this neglected period in the history of computer games that gaming was established as a cultural practice.

Gaming would not have been forced into being simply by the physical presence of computer game programs.[1] Cultural ground had to be prepared in order that people could recognize them as games and the machines that hosted them as objects to be played with. The degraded status of especially adult play in modern societies, discussed in the previous chapter, meant that computer games had to struggle for recognition and cultural space. People and places had to be prepared for their arrival. A good illustration is provided by the case of *Computer Space* (1971), the first arcade machine, which failed to garner significant player or public interest. Malliet and de Meyer attribute this to the fact that 'the instructions were too complicated', so that 'the public massively ignored *Computer Space*' (Malliet and de Meyer 2005: 25). They compare it with Bushnell's more successful tennis game, *Pong* (1972), which had just a single line of on-screen instructions[2] and is usually credited with kick-starting the modern, commercial computer games industry. As we saw in the previous chapter, the accessibility of game programs was an important factor in their success.

However, if we compare the instructions that appeared with *Computer Space* with those for contemporary console games, we can see that this is not the whole story. The enormously popular *Streetfighter* 4 (2009), for example, comes with a 43-page booklet outlining character moves and relating back-stories, while the booklet for *Dead or Alive* 4 (2005) has 39 pages, 20 of which are devoted to character backstories. This kind of extensive documentation is very common. Clearly, the problem *Computer Space* faced was not that its instructions were 'complicated' in any straightforward sense. Rather, the game's failure was due to a lack of preparation in the wider culture. Put simply, no one knew what to expect from a computer game or how to behave in connection with one. The unspoken, informal and generic rules for encountering, playing and mastering such a game had not been established. For this to happen, there had to be a new opening in the culture where computer games could be recognized and criticized. A new discourse was created around games and gaming that enabled people to make sense of the new objects and of themselves and their own activities in connection with them. To borrow a phrase from Pierre Bourdieu (1995), gaming had to be established as a cultural field, in which perceptions and dispositions are aligned with objects and identities and through which a new cultural proving ground is created.

Such a field was necessary to create people equipped to perceive certain machines as games and with the habituated dispositions and inclinations necessary to play them, that is, a gamer *habitus*. Such people possess the embodied perceptions and skills necessary to play games. They recognize themselves in gaming discourse and they use that discourse to make sense of their own practices. In this way they identify themselves with the activity. This chapter describes the development of gaming as a cultural field in this sense, by analysing the representation of games, gaming and gamers that we find in gaming magazines of the 1980s and 1990s. The argument advanced here builds on my earlier work (Kirkpatrick 2012), in which I argued that we can discern the formation of a new discursive field in the magazines of this era.

The first section describes the structural transformation of discourse about games and gaming that occurred in the mid-1980s, with particular focus on the category of gameplay. Gameplay is the central term of game evaluation and it continues to hold centre-stage in game reviews as well as much of the scholarly literature about computer games. The concept was introduced in the mid-1980s and from this time on we can see a pronounced shift in the way that games are talked about and understood, reflecting the emergence of gaming as a distinct, quasi-autonomous field within the culture. This transformation is manifest most clearly in the review sections of 1980s gaming magazines. Perturbations here, on the surface of gaming discourse, are indicative of the emergence of a new 'possibility space' (Bourdieu 1995) in the culture. The idea of 'gameplay' starts to appear in discussions of games, so for the first time game appraisal focuses on the distinctive experiences and practices of the player.

The next section focuses on the discourse around the player himself, who is increasingly identified as male, young and different from other computer users. Here too we find surface inscriptions that belie a deeper shift in the way that games are thought about and understood. Players, initially described as members of the 'computing fraternity', become 'gamesters' and then 'gamers'. Gamers have the gaming *habitus*, which means they no longer need to be told the basic principles of game operation. Gamer identity is positive in the sense that it involves expert knowledge and virtuoso performance, but it also involves what Bourdieu calls 'symbolic violence'. Older people, females and technology enthusiasts are all excluded. From the mid-1980s gaming is a more aggressive cultural presence that is avowedly not the same as computing, and the gamer is a transgressive figure, not dissimilar to the members of musical subcultures in previous decades.

These transformations mark out a new presence in the culture, a space within which games and gaming make a new kind of sense for the people who use them and, ultimately, for the rest of society as well. However, gaming's field fails to secure full autonomy in the Bourdieusian sense. Gaming discourse does not develop the kind of extended vocabulary that we associate with, for example, fine arts or literature. This is related to the fact that the legitimacy of gaming does not secure full recognition from the wider culture. Like certain sports or forms of dance, computer gaming remains problematic, vaguely transgressive and at times a cause for concern in the mainstream media. The final section of this chapter concentrates on the tensions that mark this eruption of gaming into the culture. Gamer identity is defined by the presence within it of unresolved contradictions associated with the form: it is poised uncomfortably between technology and art; it is neither childish nor adult; and it is both therapeutic and unhealthily addictive. The recuperative benefits of gamer identity must be seen alongside what Jennifer Ann Hill (2011) calls the 'importation of *faux* values', associated with the authentic gamer identity, to youthful masculinity. I suggest that there is a kind of cynicism at work here that is largely resonant with the new spirit of capitalism but which can, at times, present a challenge to dominant forces in the gaming industry.

1. The Discovery of 'Gameplay'

When gaming 'ended' in the United States, many people, including many who had enjoyed the games, were not surprised. Computer games had been derided as a fad and the rapidity with which they had become prominent perhaps made the form vulnerable to this rhetorical enframing. However, the same pattern was not repeated everywhere. In the United Kingdom and other European countries, for example, the move away from consoles was offset by the growing market for home computers, which, although more expensive than gaming machines, had always been more popular there than dedicated games machines. Officially, the small computers, many of them manufactured in the US, were educational tools that middle-class parents bought to ensure their children had an advantage in the technological future. Unofficially, however, they were gaming machines (Haddon 1988; Selwyn 2002, 2003). While in America home computers tended to lie unused in cupboards because no one knew what they were for, people in the UK and elsewhere, especially children, took to Commodores and Spectrums and used them, no doubt, for a variety of purposes, but mainly to play games.

The UK merits particular attention in this context, then, because of what has come to be known as its 'bedroom coder' culture (Newman 2004). Small computers had been sold there from early on in the 'computer revolution', starting in 1978 with the Commodore PET and Apple II, both from the US, and followed by the indigenous Cambridge MK14, a forerunner of Clive Sinclair's Spectrum machines[3] (Lean 2004). In the late 1970s and early 1980s, Commodore machines accounted for about 80 per cent of UK home computers

(Bagnall 2010: 194). In the early 1980s there were countless small developers all over the UK producing games on cassette tape and floppy disc for the diverse range of home computers. According to Izushi and Aoyama, 'Six to seven thousand titles were estimated to have been produced for the Sinclair ZX Spectrum, and more than ten thousand titles for the Commodore 64 worldwide' (Izushi and Aoyama 2006: 1852).

Computers at this time were still challenging machines with counter-intuitive, even technically demanding interfaces. To work out what to do with them, their owners consulted the magazines published to accompany them. Computing and gaming magazines were published at this time in the UK and they sold all over Europe and in Australasia.[4] As Mia Consalvo (2008) has pointed out, enthusiast magazines were central to the formation of gaming as a legitimate cultural practice.[5] However, her research focuses on US magazines of the late 1980s and early 1990s, which is after the dominant discursive constructions of gaming practice had been established. The cultural field around gaming was formed earlier and it contains unresolved tensions that leave their traces in the subsequent development of the medium. It was through the production and dissemination of words, texts and images that people's ideas about computer games were formed, making it possible for the practice of playing the games to become widespread.

The most prominent magazine of the era was *Computer and Video Games* (CVG), which commenced publication in 1981 and ran continuously until 1995. Others were formally dedicated to specific machines, including *Commodore User* (CU), which ran from 1983 to 1990, and *Zzap!*, a magazine also aimed primarily at Commodore owners that ran between 1985 and 1992. The magazines were rarely as tailored to specific computers as their names (and ownership[6]) sometimes imply, however. They all contained discussions of arcade games and games for other computers. They were also about computing, which at that time included articles about technical hardware issues and guidance on programming projects. On average, around 25 per cent of magazine content in the early years of the decade was devoted to game programs readers could copy into one of the small computers of the day.

Commodore, who made the biggest-selling home computer of the 1980s, the C64, were ambivalent in the promotion of their machine, sometimes presenting it as a games machine, at others emphasizing it could perform more serious operations perhaps useful to businesses. Where the company placed the emphasis seems often to have been partly a function of what the competition were doing (Bagnall 2010). It is worth remembering that in the 1980s companies like Atari and even Nintendo,[7] now firmly associated with gaming, also marketed other machines with more serious, home computing-type functions. The magazines reflect this context, with even CVG carrying articles on computing and programming devoid of any particular games emphasis. However, all the magazines acquired a strong focus on games within their first few issues, and they were all involved in a process of feeling their way towards a discrete gaming culture.

In early issues of the magazines, for example, there is no established way to discuss or assess games. Even recognizing a game program was not straightforward. One reviews section includes a typist training program, on the basis that 'someone might enjoy learning to type'. The pleasures specific to gaming were not yet distinguished and thematized. A vocabulary of game evaluation was something the magazines had to invent. The magazines bear witness to the struggle to make this discursive innovation. On occasion, reviewers even turn ethnographers, going out into arcades to observe and listen in on players. In CVG January 1982, a reviewer describes how they listened to people playing *Defender* (1980) to see if there was a specific gaming argot in formation. The conclusion is negative: 'it is a sign of the concentration required to play *Defender* that very few sayings connected with the game were brought to our attention', though they did apparently hear the phrase 'mountain hugging'. It took time for the key concepts of game criticism to be formulated and for the notion of 'gameplay' and related evaluative categories to emerge.

The establishment of a distinctive way of appraising games required that they be forced into view as something more than technical artefacts; as a discrete class of objects that have a unique technological dimension but are not defined by it.

Editorial and comment pieces frequently set out the standards that were applied in game reviews. From the beginning there was an effort to establish some kind of consistency by providing lists of four or five criteria that could be applied to all games. CVG's initial categories show reviewers feeling their way towards a full-fledged gaming discourse. In an early issue (September 1983), they define the criteria used in game reviews, under the heading 'How we judge the games', as follows:

> The four marks on our reviews pages are all out of a possible 10.
>
> *Getting started* refers not only to how easily it loads but the way the instructions are given and how quickly a newcomer can understand the game.
>
> *Graphics* gives marks for realism and use of the machine's capabilities to give a pleasing effect.
>
> *Playability* is the all-important question of game balance, how long it will take to build your attention and how addictive it is.
>
> *Value* takes into account the packaging, presentation and how much a player will get value for money out of the tape.

In each case, barring playability, we see that evaluative criteria for the experience of playing the games vie with more technical assessments of their qualities. *Getting started* is a category that includes technical usability, documentation issues and loading times, as well as the experience of being able to get into a game. *Graphics* are assessed for their ability to create an illusion essential to enjoyment, but also as a programming task to be accomplished within known technical parameters, while the *value* of the game seems to concern the appearance of the game as a commodity and its comparative scale as a programming project relative to other game programs. *Playability* alone is exclusively focused on the experience of the player. The attempt to clarify this idea, with use of terms like 'balance', 'attention' and 'addictiveness' mark first steps onto the ground of a properly autonomous evaluation, assessing the game from the standpoint of the player as someone who plays and not as an amateur programmer or someone who is interested in its technical properties. Enlargement of this ground is the key to the autonomy of gaming discourse.[8]

The turning point in this history and certainly the most significant conceptual-linguistic innovation is the category of 'gameplay'. This idea has been the principal contribution of computer gaming discourse to contemporary cultural reflection and is widely taken as marking the difference between computer games and older games (which also had to secure and hold our attention). Gameplay is the aesthetic category that distinguishes computer games in the history of media, and it signals to the wider culture that something new and different has arrived. Its introduction into discussion and analysis of games marks a kind of rupture or break that establishes a new field of discourse with its own, unique set of questions and its own principles. When gameplay is taken for granted as the primary concept of game evaluation, this signifies the presence of a new cultural field, within which playing computer games and assigning value to the activity now make sense on their own terms, not as training for something else or as part of a technical procedure.

The two terms, game and play, were first placed together in the distinctive formation 'game play', without contraction, in magazine reviews from 1983. However, from mid-1985, the contracted form becomes the norm and starts to be used much more frequently in reviews and discussions in all the magazines. In the April 1985 issue of CU over the course of two short reviews, the author of the 'Screen Scene' section introduces the phrase 'game play' first to describe a game for the Commodore 64 called *Cauldron*. The game involves 'you play[ing] the part of a witch seeking the golden broomstick'. To achieve this goal the player collects ingredients from around the game to make a magic spell. The reviewer praises the game for being easy to get into: 'Cauldron is one of those games where you can just pick up the joystick and play'. At the same time, though, the game 'is the most cunningly planned' game he has come across for some time, so it is not too easy. The review concludes: 'It's impossible to fault Cauldron. They've got everything right. Splendid graphics, interesting plot, and above all challenging and entertaining game play'. The next review is for an adventure game, also for the Commodore computer, called *Shadowfire*. What's interesting about this game is that it is described as 'a text adventure without text'. Instead of entering directional commands in the form of 'east', 'west' on the keyboard, players used their joysticks to 'simply move an on-screen cursor to an icon which represents the required action. Press fire and the command is implemented'. The reviewer (correctly) expresses confidence that 'we will see this technique used a lot more in the future'. The effect of the new control is that '*Shadowfire* creates a total atmosphere that gamers can lose themselves in – the essence of a good adventure. The revolutionary icon gameplay technique is the icing on the cake'. Here the hyphenated form of the phrase marks the arrival of the key concept in video game criticism, one which has held sway over the tastes of gamers for the subsequent three and a half decades. Far from being 'icing on the cake', the revolutionary control mechanism, which the author links to what we would now call the game's immersive properties, is associated with a linguistic innovation whose meaning marks a decisive rupture, the structural transformation of gaming discourse.

From this point on, the concept of gameplay begins to constitute the philosopher's stone of gaming: it is the enigmatic mark of value that producers compete over. Making a game with good gameplay is every designer's goal to this day. At the same time, there were initially no clear criteria with which to measure its presence. The fact that there was no stable consensus over what the compound noun actually signified reflects the fact that, just as Bourdieu (2009) says in relation to *form* in art, it is both a stake in the game and the decisive move made by winners. Successful game designers produced games with gameplay and, in persuading players this was what they had done, they determined the signification of the term. The meanings of 'gameplay' are determined in the struggles of players to understand and appraise their experiences. The semantics of gameplay turn on the way that the term is deployed, not only in the reviews in the magazines but also in the culture beyond. Its introduction is symptomatic of the arrival of a new discursive ordering that regulates the sense that people can make of their activity as game players. It also represents the presence of a new recuperative possibility. Subjective tastes and preferences can be reflected upon and shared beyond the reach of, and occasionally even in opposition to, game producers. The demand for good gameplay, expressed through letters pages and reviews, applies pressure on games companies to create authentic products – games for gamers.

Gaming discourse secures its autonomy partly by articulating gameplay as a term that is *opposed* to other elements of gaming experience. Previously, playability, and even game play in the non-contracted form, sat alongside other criteria in a review of a game: those terms were not opposed to other features. For example, in the first issue of CU, we read that a game called '*Sheepdog* is not very realistic, but basically a good game', and that 'great graphics don't make a playable game'. After 1985, such contrasts take on a different, more aggressive inflection. Now gameplay is opposed to things like graphics, character, plot and so on. As well as being the mark of a good game for reviewers, gameplay also signifies the tastes and preferences of a new subject, namely, the authentic gamer. The true gamer, as we will see below, is the player who is interested in *games* and not computers; *gameplay* and not stories, and graphics in so far as they *reward* good, skilful play. This inflection is the key to the autonomy of the field, but its inherently negative, antagonistic logic also tells us something about the limited and partial character of that autonomy.

2. The 'Authentic' Gamer

The transformation of gaming discourse is structural because it changes the rules that underpin our talk about games and gaming. This is what makes the term 'gameplay' mean something different after 1985, when before it was just an odd expression. Discussions of playability and of what makes a 'good' game take on a sense that they did not previously possess. From the perspective that this opens up, a class of objects called computer games looms into a special, foregrounded position while computer technology recedes. In Bourdieu's terms, this foregrounding is the primary effect of a field; the establishment of a set of determinate perceptions and dispositions that are actually constitutive for a class of objects and practices. The circulation of gaming discourse contributed to a determinate structuring of perceptions and it is through this process that what counts as a computer game has been socially and culturally determined in practice. The creation of that discourse was an effect of the radical imaginary. The modification of perceptions expressed in the changing evaluative criteria applied to games goes along with and reflects a broader change to the physiognomic dispositions of entrants to the field. Bourdieu's (1995) idea of lived *habitus* is particularly useful here.

Entrants to the field do not learn its rules primarily through a conscious process of cognitive acquisition: you cannot study to become a gamer. Those who play acquire a historically specific *habitus*, meaning that they are disposed within their own bodies in such a way that picking up a controller, and rattling keys and twisting a mouse in the specific manner associated with playing computer games, are practices that are natural and obvious to them. The modification of perception and acquisition of a unique disposition within one's own body are mediated through discourses that relate bodies and things to produce new identities. Becoming a gamer depends upon the existence of the field, but the existence of the field presupposes that there are 'gamers'. The rupture that established gaming proceeds through what Bourdieu (1995) calls *hysteresis*, or reverse causation, in which the identity 'gamer' and the field pull each other into being, with gameplay as the mediating term.

The concept of *habitus* is particularly germane to an analytics of gameplay because the mesh of human sensory and motor functions with computer interface apparatus is a complex embodied process. To draw on Thompson's (1995) terminology, players engage computer games on multiple 'medial planes'. Computer games are inserted into the human sensorium in a unique way: no other medium interfaces with human beings on so many levels at once. Games provide sounds, sights and somatic stimuli that have to be processed and responded to using eyes, hands and other parts of the body. In a short period of historical time, gamers have habituated themselves to the special kinds of performance necessary to accommodate and respond to these new objects. Moreover, while the basic dispositions of using controllers, scrutinizing screens and taking in sounds are relatively constant, the rules of these performances are subject to change between games and often require deliberation as well as intuitive or habituated physical responses. Players' embodied experiences with games involve complex engagements with multiple, intersecting planes of sensory information. While games have cinematic and story elements and to some extent these may organize players' activity, perhaps inclining them to do this rather than that at specific points in the action, the processing of game information is an embodied skill that has to be learned. As Shigeru Miyamoto, designer of numerous games including *Donkey Kong* and the *Zelda* series put it, 'you feel what fun the game is with your entire body' (cited in Kline et al. 2003: 118).

Players internalize, or habituate themselves to, a repertoire of controller operations that includes the perceptual orientation to games as specific ensembles of equipment, including a controller whose precise manner of operation will be configured specifically for each game, yet whose core principles are standard for the medium. Henrik Smed Nielsen puts this well when he writes that 'playing computer games requires my embodiment of the game's material artefacts – I have to master the game's controls' (Nielsen 2010: 27). Nielsen's analysis also emphasizes that the game's feedback, often equated to its visual element, is actually multi-sensory, ranging from rumble controllers to interesting uses of sound and music in which effects are calibrated to player action.

As computer games have differentiated into genres (action games, role-playing games, first person shooters, etc.), so the gamer *habitus* has diversified into what Andreas Gregersen calls a plurality of 'interaction modes'. He writes that 'the overall set of embodied skills for interacting with technology is a crucial part of the genre repertoire of agents in a given community: gamers know their games and the requisite success criteria and they also know specific interfaces and the requisite interaction modes' (2011: 101). As far as games are concerned, the very meaning of distinctions like those of genre, normally associated with fictional content, are powerfully conditioned by the nature of the game's 'interactive mode'. Adventure and puzzle games, for example, are highly deliberative but they still require more than just thought for their operation. Action genres and first person shooters present planes of engagement that intersect hands and eyes, demanding more dynamic embodied responses.

The relationship of gameplay to conventional interpretation – the rules for making sense of established media – are complex and at times strained, making player involvement all the more intriguing and, of course, all the more in need of its own field, in which the rules that determine the coherence of the activity and sort it for evaluative purposes are codified. The wide diffusion and popularity of gaming is evidence of extensive cultural work, and this work is necessary because playing a computer game is not at all like other cultural pursuits such as watching television or even playing a board game.

The mode of embodiment specific to gaming begins to be rendered intelligible, thematized in gaming discourse, in the course of the break referred to in the previous section. This is evident in the magazines and especially the way they present games in reviews. The relevant change is most clear in the kinds of description that mediate the player's relationship to their on-screen character. In magazines of the early 1980s, it is not uncommon to read descriptions like the following: 'the player is in charge of a marker at the bottom of the screen', or, in a discussion of *Pac-Man 2*: 'the player controls the munchman using his keyboard' (CVG, 3 January 1982, pp. 30, 72). In another example from 1983, a racing game is described in the following terms: 'Each player chooses a lane and tries to advance the symbol in that lane' (CU, 1 October 1983, p. 44). What is striking about these early reviews to the contemporary reader is the way that they guide readers into making a connection between their actions and the behaviour of the game program by explicitly identifying which game elements they control. References to 'your little man' are common. Once the structural transformation referred to above has occurred, reviewers assume that players intuit this connection without the need for any such guidance. In magazines after the break, players are simply told, 'you play as a worm', or 'you are driving a rig' (CVG 169, December 1995). From the mid-1980s, as the idea of gameplay takes hold, the way that operating games is described changes, so that increasingly a near-symbiotic fusion of the two terms (game and player) is assumed. Game reviews from later in the decade assume that players know how to play.

The discovery of 'gameplay' is the moment at which the body of the gamer closes around the gaming apparatus to make it invisible, so that the characteristic sensations of gameplay can form the basis of gaming's appeal. Gameplay, like the pleasure of art appreciation, is difficult to justify through the power of sharper definition or more refined argument (cf. Leino 2012). The concept is elusive: you either get it or you don't. In Bourdieu's (2009) terms, this is gaming's unspoken *illusio*. By the time we get to the late 1980s, players are physically attuned to the activity of playing games, and gameplay serves as both the core evaluative concept in game criticism and as the mark of authenticity in gaming identity. The true gamer is the one who understands and appreciates good gameplay *from within* and the 'gamer's game' is the one that has it in abundance.

The identity 'gamer' was formed in this coming together of a gaming *habitus* with the new discursive formation that made sense of games in terms of the thrills of 'gameplay'. The gamer is an effect of the structural transformation of gaming discourse and this effect of the radical imaginary is also clear in the magazines. In writing about games in the early 1980s, there is no mention of 'gamers' – the term and the discrete class of individuals it signifies did not yet exist. Initially gaming magazines understood and addressed their readers as members of the 'computing fraternity'. But, as indicated above, a primary effect of gaming's field is to distance games from computers in the wider sense. Moving towards 1985, other expressions are experimented with, including 'gamesters', whose slightly diminutive connotations reflect the fact that the magazines are still aimed at parents and children, with the latter being more likely to play. With the discovery of gameplay and the opening up of gaming's cultural space, readers are addressed as 'gamers' for the first time. This signals a new confidence about the target constituency for games. Ultimately, it is a contributing factor in determining the kinds of games that get produced as well, a theme to which I return in the next chapter.

Gaming's field positions play with computer games as a cultural practice in relation to other activities. In so doing, it accommodates some 'position-takings' as acceptable for gamers and prohibits others. The gamer is one who appreciates gameplay and knows what makes a good game, but such a person must also possess other attributes. As gamer identity takes root, games become particularly associated with youth and with a particular kind of masculinity. Dmitri Williams has pointed out that 'During the mid-1980s and the 1990s, video games were constructed as the province of children . . . the popular conception of game use as a purely child-centric phenomenon did not emerge until well after gaming had entered the popular consciousness' (D. Williams n.d.: 13–14).

This change can be seen in the voice of the magazines, which in the early 1980s is often parental. The first issue of CVG (1981), for example, reviews a chess game and addresses itself to the adult who is likely to buy such a device: 'This offers a good game to the keen chess youngster who is short of an opponent . . . it will also fit into most family budgets' (p. 25), while a year later a review describes a game as one that will keep 'the whole family entertained'. An advert in the November 1983 issue proclaims that 'As your children get bigger so can your Atari 2600'. These formulations rationalize the adult purchase of computers. When game reviews address young readers directly, they often do so in a condescending way, as in the review that says: 'We've been telling you vidkids out there just how good that old-fashioned arcade game pinball is for some time now' (CVG 25, November 1983, p. 48). The magazines often seek to educate, even about games and play, and the position this confers upon young readers is occasionally embraced in the all-important letters pages, with one young correspondent writing in the January 1982 edition that 'As a beginner I look forward to buying the magazine regularly'. The early magazines do occasionally talk up the 'fun' aspects of games and extol their virtues in terms of 'addictiveness' and 'violence', in ways that might be expected to unsettle parents looking for wholesome 'family entertainment' and 'educational' values, but this is not their dominant tone.

Later magazines address their readers more assuredly as teenage, male gamers. We move from a mode of address in which parents are supervising and gamers are their children to one in which young people are the sole intended audience. Significantly, the appearance of gaming magazines starts to change as well, so that by the 1990s they look more like boys' comics. In the 1990s magazines, it is common to find that game imagery actually obscures text in the reviews. The authentic gamer is still avowedly young but he is not a child. A review in CVG 171 (February 1996) of *Namco Museum: Volume One* (1995), which made arcade classics available for the Playstation, contains numerous derogatory references to older people: 'old duffers', we are told, will 'rejoice' in being able to play the games again and they are also referred to as 'old sods' (these players would have been in the their late 20s or early 30s at the time). Similarly, in the November 1995 issue (p. 48) there is a negative reference to 'the kinds of maths your dad might like'. Significantly, trainspotters, games workshop enthusiasts and even 'board games heads' are all condemned as 'dull' (CVG 168, November 1995, p. 22). These statements are distancing strategies, and their effect is to differentiate the gamer from other identities, especially those people who just a few years earlier had all been members of the same 'computing fraternity'.[9] Through these negative relations, gamer identity takes on a kind of weight of its own, enabling aggressive assertions of positive presence, like the reference to the fact that 'even the women behind the counter of WH Smith's have heard of Playstations now' (CVG 168, November 1995, p. 52).

The emergence of a new 'gamer' identity is directly related to the structural shift in gaming discourse discussed above. The authentic gamer opposes gameplay to story and other varieties of frippery in games. 'Sad fops', we are told in a review of a fighting game, get taken in by good-looking moves when what really matters is their effectiveness in intense gameplay (CVG 168, November 1995, p. 37). Being an authentic gamer involves being 'cool', liking the right music and being a practising virtuoso of gameplay performance. 'It's a mark of cool to master this game', states a CVG review of *Ridge Racer* in February 1996. As well as positioning gamers by distancing them from some uncool activities and linking them to other, usually rebellious ones, gaming discourse distinguishes the real gamer from the 'fop', the one who 'gets it' from people other youth cultures might have characterized as posers or fakers.[10] An appreciation of and facility for gameplay here becomes the key to accumulating what Consalvo (2008) calls 'gaming capital': there is an established constituency for games with rules for securing recognition and affording esteem, and these things can be accumulated. Understanding good gameplay is the mark of a real gamer and it opposes them to the 'uncool'. We can confidently assert that writing to CVG and describing oneself as 'a beginner' would not have given one much of this precious commodity in the late 1980s or early 1990s scene.

Although games are now assessed on terms that are independent of computing in a wider sense, the authentic gamer still knows his technology. Especially after the revival of consoles in the second half of the 1980s, however, technological knowledge is deployed in a different way. In place of representations that place detailed technical descriptions (or pages of code, which made up about one third of each magazine in the early 1980s) alongside other features, like story or plot, in later reviews technical references take on a different function. In the November 1995 issue of CVG, for instance, 16-bit consoles are described as 'a bit crappy' (pp. 34–5) and the reviewer of *Rayman* (1995) jokes that the game is only worth having if you have a *Jaguar* console (because there were few games for that 64-bit machine). The author rejects the game on the grounds that it makes little use of the benefits of the 32-bit machines of the day, unlike other games such as *Super-Mario 2: Yoshi's Island* (1995). The issue here is not that more powerful consoles are straightforwardly better, as the reference to the *Jaguar* shows, but rather that some machines are the current standard, the norm within the gaming community, and that games should be designed to be compatible with them and to get the most out of them. This is defined in terms of novelty (getting them to do new things) and 'reward': a nebulous concept that depends upon the successful formation of gaming's *illusio* in the intervening years.

As the disparaging references to women in WH Smith's indicates, the shift described here also marks the time when gaming began to disregard female players. The gamer is a young male. Gaming discourse announces its presence with a certain swagger, denouncing those who don't 'get' gameplay, and deriding those who still need explanations. It is true that there were always computer games that involved sex and were sometimes sexist. In terms of overt narrative content, the earliest years of gaming present several examples of games that try to persuade would-be buyers of their pornographic content. One of the first examples of such a game was *The Naughty One* (1983), made to run on Atari and Apple machines. In this game, nudity is the theme. Players try to 'win' their opponent's clothes while keeping their own. Seduction is dramatized as a constant threat to keeping one's dignity. Adverts for *The Naughty One* stressed that the game was about the sleazy side of life, with reference to 'massage parlours' (the phrase was a euphemism for brothels in the UK at this time) and dodgy dealings with pawn brokers (who would buy your clothes). Similarly, in 1983, a software publisher called Knightsoft sold a game called *Strip Poker* and adverts for this game show a cartoon woman viewed from the perspective of a leering, cigar-holding male: the game tries to position itself within the seedier recesses of 1980s middle-class male culture. An editorial in one of the magazines refers to a developer whose products had to be sold in 'plain brown wrappers'.

It would be wrong, however, to view these examples as part of a continuous history of the association of games with misogyny or sexism. This point bears emphasis: gaming became sexist and female players were rendered more or less invisible by the structural transformation of gaming's discourse and the relocation of gaming in its own field. One reason it is easy to find sexist games from the period before the break is the sheer number of games that were produced. In the early 1980s, game makers experimented with topics as diverse as being unemployed in Hampstead, gardening, even housework, as well as the more standard science fiction themes and moments of pure abstraction. In fact, the magazines show that the discourse around games was markedly more prone to reflection on gender issues in the years prior to 1985. In CU 20 (May 1985, p. 68), for example, in an article on the 'rescue the princess' theme common to many games then and now, we find reflection on the sexist implications of the narrative. A month earlier (CU 19, April 1985, p. 41), a review criticized a game for its lack of female characters. In CVG 9, July 1982, there is a whole article on recent games aimed at women (p. 73), while the following month a 'women's perspective' is offered on games, although this largely bemoans their appeal to men which, it says, creates 'computer widows' (CVG 10, p. 13). To be sure, these are mainly isolated remarks that rarely become extended lines of reflection, but it is difficult to imagine them appearing in magazines later in the decade, when the gender identity of gamers has been firmly consolidated.[11] By the late 1980s, for example, letters to CVG are no longer addressed politely to the editor but to a character called 'Yob', whose comments are routinely sexist and rest on the tacit assumption that he has no female correspondents.[12]

3. Gaming's Constitutive Ambivalence

The burgeoning gamer identity marks out a negative symbolic boundary, then, that excludes computer obsessives, older people and females. Gamers appreciate gameplay and are good at it; they are young, male and 'cool'. The gamer identity must be seen as an accomplishment of the cultural work referred to at the beginning of this chapter. It is the most striking product of gaming's bid for cultural autonomy, for recognition as a valid cultural practice independent of other technical practices and possessing its own, internal criteria for evaluating games and play. The gamer subject position reflects a positive presence in the culture, a place that allows people to rationalize the pleasure they take in an activity with reference to an imagined community who share their values. Within this community, good gameplay is esteemed and games are discussed and criticized. Viewed in this way, becoming an authentic gamer affords some respite from the demands of work and the machinations of the consumerist culture industry. Gaming is a cultural activity with values and rules that are communicatively transmitted and discussed. At the same time, however, it reflects the entanglement of human beings in a cultural practice that is not fully autonomous. This *quasi*-autonomy of gaming is important to understanding where the activity stands in relation to the larger sociological questions that motivate the current work.

The gaming community sets rules for authentic participation and uses symbolic violence to carve out a new, exclusive social space. It is also, however, a place where people can secure recognition for their achievements. Gaming is normally a competitive activity and it makes sense that people derive satisfaction from performing well. As Boltanski and Chiapello (2005) point out, achievement and fulfilment require validation of what is accomplished in a community:

> Self-fulfillment possesses meaning only as the achievement of something. Yet, however diverse the things it might tend towards, it nevertheless remains dependent upon the existence of ends that are worth fulfilling . . . these ends cannot be purely individual; in order to be legitimate and worth the sacrifices they demand, they must be inscribed in a collective. (Boltanski and Chiapello 2005: 432)

In a time when employment is often in short-lived projects and careers are fragmented and have to be reflexively negotiated, with more and more of the costs associated with this (including the psychological costs) borne by individuals, finding recognition for one's achievements in non-work contexts becomes more important. It is increasingly vital to be able to recuperate one's sense of self and self-worth in a context that is not controlled by the demands of work. Studies of consumption in the era of networked capitalism have suggested that this is something people tend to do by joining informal communities based on the consumption of particular kinds of goods or media (Jenkins 2006a; Zukin 2004). Entering gaming culture, becoming a gamer, is a recuperative strategy in this sense. Here it is important that games and play are *not* a transient phenomenon of popular culture but a very concrete institution that perdures, perhaps one that is essential to networked capitalism.

As such, gaming and the gamer identity include contradictions touched on earlier. As I indicated previously, identities constructed through engagement with commodities, mass-produced artefacts sold for profit often by large corporations, are points of vulnerability for individuals because they result in dependency. This is not simply a matter of the capriciousness of game producers, who may just discontinue a game, as in the case of on-line MMPGs, or not produce a sequel. It concerns the identity itself and the resources it can actually provide.[13] Analysis of its field shows that gaming identity rests on relatively thin, unstable ground. The cool, male gamer imports tensions that derive from the partial character of gaming's bid for cultural autonomy, tensions that are still visible in contemporary gaming culture.

The structural transformation of gaming discourse foregrounds games and gaming, separating them out from computer technology in general and, as we have seen, opening up space in which the gamer becomes something different from and even opposed to the technology obsessive. This involves creating an idea of games and of their qualities as irreducible to their character as computer programs. However, even after the invention of gameplay and the development of a more autonomous evaluative discourse, these issues are not fully resolved. Gaming's bid for autonomy stalls. Despite the rhetorical emphasis placed in the early magazines on freeing up players' imagination and on the potential of what is perceived as a new medium – the first CVG editorial, for instance, declares that the magazine 'is out to push your imagination to the limits' – it seems they quickly encountered, or perhaps set themselves, new discursive limitations.

This is illustrated by the November 1995 issue of CVG (168). The editorial for this issue describes staff changes to the magazine and relates them to a new orientation within the magazine. The industry, it says, is now a 'serious business' and 'gamers demand more sophisticated titles'. Pursuant to this, the magazine promises 'more ruthless . . . comments and ratings' to help players secure the best products. However, a few pages further on, in a review of *Guardian Heroes*, a game for the Sega Saturn console, the reviewer announces that the game is 'hard to describe'. It and the following two reviews largely lapse into a discussion of different 'boards', falling back into a technical appraisal, although, as noted in the previous section, this is not a detailed analysis but a rhetorical strategy that positions the games reviewed in relation to the contemporary hardware environment, that is, it marks them as 'up to the minute', or as deviations from the contemporary trajectory. Paradoxically, there is an emphasis here on the increased complexity of new games, so that one review comments that 'the volume of new or improved features is phenomenal' (pp. 24–5, review of Konami ISS football game), but little corresponding differentiation of the critical discourse to be applied to them.

This faltering character of gaming discourse suggests that it encounters an internal limit on its autonomy and is indicative of its failure really to secure full, unproblematic legitimacy for computer gaming as a new cultural practice. Since this has not limited the development of the medium, we must take it that it is constitutive of gaming that it is defined by a kind of failure, an internal limitation that prevents it from becoming, like art, a fully autonomous cultural practice. Instead, its discourse is curiously stymied. Gaming only secures recognition as a cultural practice when it is opposed to technology, yet gaming discourse continues to rely on technical allusion to describe its objects. It is as if every aesthetic comparison of Mozart to Beethoven was obliged to discuss the innovations made to brass instruments in the years between their creative lives. The development of gaming's distinctive evaluative criteria and a language for game appraisal stalls.

Aside from gameplay itself, the most common way of assessing a game's quality is in terms of its 'addictiveness'. The ambiguity of this term is highly suggestive. Through the use of this kind of terminology, gaming discourse exhibits a recurrent concern with the normalcy of gaming practice and testifies to an enduring lack of self-confidence within gaming discourse. This remains the case even in the contemporary gaming press. This ambivalence is constitutive for gaming, by which I mean that the position it has established for itself in the culture is of a practice that is not normal but not really pathological either. A good game treads this boundary well by being dangerously compulsive, mind-bending even, but not so extreme that no one would want to do it. Even the messages about how some games contain sequences that may prompt seizures should be seen in this context: games are always inherently risky, yet completely safe.

Just as games have only quasi-autonomous principles of aesthetic as against technological evaluation, so their appeal involves the notion of childhood, itself undergoing various kinds of change since the 1980s, and of transgression. Indeed, settling on the adolescent male of this period as its target audience means being both childish and unsettling to ideas of childhood. As ambivalent as it is in this way, the computer game contributes to a change in the culture that sees children less as passive recipients of cultural messages and more as collaborators and participants in their creation. Jennifer Hill argues that 'one of the more significant outcomes' of the growth of consumerism has been 'the steady and relentless erosion of childhood' (2011: 348), so that the institution 'at least as we know it in the West, is fading out altogether' (2011: 349).[14] As children assume more responsibility for important consumer choices like consoles and expensive game programs to play on them, so they are inducted into a world without innocence.

Noting the salience of negative behaviours in prevailing ideas of 'cool',[15] Hill suggests that 'Consumerism fosters a culture that tolerates the negation of positive self-image by attaching *faux* values to the core of an individual's identity' (2011: 350), an observation with clear implications for games and games marketing, which often emphasizes themes of violence and has, at least since the mid-1990s, played on ambiguity between youthful appeal and adult content (Kline et al. 2003). Computer games are for young people but they are inherently transgressive and troubling to prevailing ideas about childhood. Games are toys – they are still associated with fun and play – but they are also harder than this. Now allied to other parts of teenage culture, it is clear that there are people who will never 'get' games because they are too old, too female or just 'uncool'. Gameplay itself has become a social sorting concept, central to the unequal distribution of gaming capital, which is a hard, grown-up currency only available to children and the lack of which only young people experience as a deprivation. Here we see a third constitutive ambivalence in gaming culture, namely, that computer games aspire to be more than just childish playthings, but they do not for all that ever succeed in being 'grown up'. Gaming is here constituted by its stymied autonomy from childish concerns and from childhood as the appropriate location for play in the culture. It strives to become, and even succeeds in being, something more than that, but when it succeeds it stops being a game.

In part, these limitations of gaming's field reflect the historical status of games in the time before computer gaming, discussed in the previous chapter. In this context, reference to games, including the idea that everything might 'be just a game' finds resonances in the affected nonchalance of teenage culture. In part, the collapse of critical thought in the 1990s reflects the insertion of a kind of ubiquitous levity as a stand-in for social revolution: for 'post-modernism' the pretensions of old institutions are deflated as no one really believes in anything any more. This new order fosters cynicism (Sloterdijk 1987) and, as I have argued elsewhere (Kirkpatrick 2004, 2011), the attitude of seeing through appearances and recognizing their illusory character while doing nothing to change their underlying causes is integral to the aesthetics of play with computer games. Gamers know the real value of their accomplishments with games and consequently gaming as a field is shot through with a strange irony. However, whatever its strengths as a survival strategy, cynicism only works within strict limits. Living in 'pretend mode' can help people adjust temporarily, but it cannot work 'for long' (Boltanski and Chiapello 2005: 376, 459). The identity 'gamer' is one that few people wear in complete seriousness. This highlights its significance as a point of volatility within contemporary culture and, of course, feeds back into its continuing status as vaguely transgressive. If the cynicism of the cool gamer is a *'faux value'*, then we might be forgiven for asking what the correct values are – the ones that we really ought to have as subjects of the new spirit of capitalism.

CHAPTER FOUR

Technology and Power

Gaming's bid to be taken, if not seriously, then at least on its own terms, resulted in a popular perception of computer games as inherently troublesome. In this way their boundary status has become constitutive, so that a game that does not spark some kind of controversy (too original to be just a game; too violent for children; too addictive to be healthy) tends to be refused recognition as a 'real' game or rejected as a poor one. Computer games have become mass market commodities, central to the contemporary, global culture industry without shaking off these connotations. Despite this and the often-declared intentions of game publishers to 'improve' their products, the association of games with controversy seems to be incorrigible.

One perspective on the failure of games to grow up and mature into a serious expressive medium lays the blame at the feet of the corporations who make them. The commercialization of games production, which snuffed out a lively experimental industry and imposed its own logic of mass production, requires products that grab attention in a crowded media marketplace. Consequently, there is a drive to produce games of a given, saleable type and this inhibits the development of their expressive capacities. The result is a degraded product that often comes loaded with negative ideological messages (Dyer-Witheford and de Peuter 2009). According to this line of argument, computer games have the capacity to be something much better, more beneficial to humanity perhaps, but capitalist commercialization inhibits and distorts that potential. In this chapter, I will suggest that this rests on an idealization of the 'potential' of games, which overlooks the constitutive role of gaming's field and its built-in tensions. As we saw in the previous chapter, the transgressive aspects of this were already in place before gaming was developed and expanded by global capital.

This chapter describes how a practice that consists in playing at the boundaries of technology/art, childhood/ violence and normalcy/addiction has become organized into a global culture industry. It casts the active participation of gamers and gaming as a relatively autonomous source of values and tastes as key elements in the development of that industry. Gamers exert pressure for 'better' games but what this means in practice may not correspond to our expectations of a new medium or cultural practice progressing to maturity.

By the mid-1990s, a new generation of gaming consoles had transformed computer games into commodities of a new, global culture industry. As indicated in chapter 1, this rise of games and gaming needs to be understood in the context of broader social and economic changes associated with the move to networked, or informational, capitalism. As Boltanski and Chiapello (2005) observe, networked capitalism involves a drastic extension of the range of things that become commodified. Computer games must be seen as part of what they refer to as a succession of 'liberating gadgets' that are associated with renewal of the excitement of capitalism (Boltanski and Chiapello 2005: 437–8). The counter-cultural longing for a more authentic existence is met through the production of commodities, even though authenticity is in part defined by the fact that it cannot be commodified (2005: 476). This perverse logic is central to the process whereby capitalism absorbs the artistic critique and changes in response to it without ceasing to be capitalism. It underlies the shift to 'virtual' commodities, which have to be instantiated or actualized by their consumers, as discussed by Lash and Lury (2007). It is in this sense that Kline et al. are right to call computer games the 'ideal commodity of informational capitalism' (2003: 24).

This chapter explores these issues first through an analysis of the organization of the games industry since the mid-1990s. The first section describes the relationships that obtain between developers, publishers and console manufacturers that make and distribute the games, describing how changes to technology have been used to standardize game production, to manage the creative process and articulate it to the global market. Focusing particularly on the role of middleware, or game engines, makes it clear how, within computer game production, the creative role of designers and developers faces off against the economic imperatives of efficient production for a competitive market, reflected in the demands of publishers and console manufacturers and embodied in technology. The core technologies of game manufacture serve particular interests, intruding on concept development and product differentiation in ways that are determinate for the quality of the resulting products. This has particular consequences for those who work in the industry, who are largely drawn to games by their own status as gamers, but who find themselves subject to new, more intrusive forms of exploitation.

The second section looks at the tension between local and global factors in the organization of computer game production. It is correct to emphasize the role of 'the playful genius of immaterial labour' (Dyer-Witheford and de Peuter 2009: 14) in the games industry, but labour should not be understood in terms of a universal 'multitude' that mirrors an abstract, global capital. Although the design and manufacture of games is a global process in which different actors are connected through 'global production networks' (Johns 2006), games are also cultural commodities, and their character necessarily reflects the influence of local variations. Important differences remain, for example, between the Japanese industry and those in the US and Europe, with implications for the quality of the goods produced. Local gaming and business cultures contribute to shaping game production, even as the logic of globalization continues to erode these differences. While globalized firms tend to handle the resulting tensions through clever advertising and the projection of iconic characters as brands, they are constrained not by the revolutionary capacities of a naked, unmediated and rebellious play but by the culture of taste whose formation was analysed in the previous chapter.

The final section in this chapter turns to reflection on the role of players in the industry. Consumers of digital products are commonly cast as 'prosumers', 'co-creators' or, in the case of games, 'playbourers' (Kucklich 2005; Sotamaa 2009) of the products they buy, because they have to work to get anything out of them. This activity raises questions about ownership, especially the legitimacy of proprietorial restrictions on the uses of game software and how these should be applied to plastic objects that to a greater or lesser extent are made what they are by the people who use them. This section examines whether the practice of modding games, creating new levels and characters out of existing programs, constitutes a kind of progressive revival of older forms of game making – a form of resistance to commodification – or is actually, as some have suggested, merely another way in which consumers are drawn into the production process, extending and deepening the new deployments of power characteristic of the gaming industry. Here gaming illustrates new dimensions of control associated with the global culture industry (Lash and Lury 2007), but it also clarifies the relation of active embodied play to a historically specific social imaginary, which is expressed through the idea of gameness and membership of the imagined community of gamers.

1. Organizing an Industry

From its subcultural roots in the mid-1980s, gaming has become a global industry with estimated annual sales at the time writing of approximately US$56 billion (*Economist* 2011),[1] projected to grow to around US$70 billion in 2013. Recent studies show that it continues to grow more rapidly than other entertainment sectors, so that while media entertainment as a whole has a projected annual growth rate of around 17 per cent, the figure for games is 70 per cent (De Prato et al. 2010: 62). The industry is dominated by three console manufacturers: Microsoft, Sony and Nintendo. Microsoft is one of the largest corporations in the world and currently derives about one fifth (approx. 18.25 per cent) of its income from its games division (Edge 2008: 56). Games programs account for 27 per cent of software produced in Japan (Aoyama and Izushi 2003: 425).

Nintendo are credited with establishing the commercial model for this success, which is based on a division of functions between console manufacturers, game publishers and developers. To prevent the kind of glut of poor-quality software that did so much harm to Atari, Nintendo imposed restrictions on which firms they would allow to make games for their new console, the Nintendo Entertainment System (NES) when they launched it in 1986, and they restricted access to their machine, effectively preventing non-approved developers from gaining access to the console market. The result was restored consumer confidence, which was especially important in the US context.[2] This model was the basis for the resurrection of computer games there after the crash discussed in chapter 2. Nintendo are estimated to have had 20–30 per cent of the global software market in the second half of the 1980s, based on the success of the NES, and 'for some five years Nintendo was synonymous with gaming' (Kline et al. 2003: 117, 125). In Europe, Sega's Megadrive[3] console, introduced in 1989, enjoyed similar success, although it was some time before console gaming would displace games played on computers.

The 1990s saw several failed attempts to enter the console market, including the Atari Jaguar (1993) and the 3DO Multiplayer. Most of these were short-lived because of a lack of games, a pattern that was repeated by the Sega Saturn (1994)

and their Dreamcast (1999) console, which was more powerful than any rival games machine and had internet connectivity. However, it was only when Sony produced the Playstation
in 1994 that Nintendo encountered a long-term rival. Although
Sony are also a Japanese firm, Nintendo's loss of monopoly
in the console market reflected the fact that games were being
produced again on a new commercial scale in North America
and Europe. Games from Japan remained popular everywhere
but their share of non-Japanese markets underwent a decline
from this time.[4]

Technological changes made game production prohibi-
tively expensive for individuals working in the 'bedroom
coder' tradition, discussed in the previous chapter. Computers in the 1980s had required technical understanding. Users
needed to know how to enter commands in a format their
machine would understand. The hours spent copying games
programs from magazines had introduced gamesters to this
way of interacting with the machine. In the early 1990s,[5]
however, there was a move within the technical community
towards the creation of interfaces that would make computers
more accessible to their human users. As the power and
capacity of home computers grew, a campaign developed
within the technical design community to present them to
people in terms that they could understand (Kirkpatrick
2004). A new group of experts associated with interface
design created screens with clickable icons and images that
people could relate to as metaphors for environments they
were familiar with in their non-computing lives, most
famously the 'desktop' (Johnson 1997). Through the new academic discipline of human–computer interaction (H-CI),
principles that had previously informed game design became
extended to computing more generally, spearheading a new
popularity for the machine.

Easy-to-use but more restrictive programs transformed
most workplaces in the course of the decade, including in
the games industry. Game production in particular was

transformed by the introduction of software development kits (SDKs), or game engines. These made the process of game design easier by offering programmers standardized modules, sometimes referred to as middleware. One effect of this was to automate the quality control process. Only someone working with a licensed SDK could write a game for a given console, while their use of the SDK ensured that the game would run well on the given machine. The introduction of game engines meant that developers could be given more autonomy from the console manufacturers. In the late 1990s, 'game developers had more freedom, a fact that was further enhanced by a whole range of programs and devices that became available to simplify programming' (Malliet and de Meyer 2005: 39). The downside of this change in the design of computer interfaces is a loss of real control for the worker. In order to parcel up computing functionality and make it available to users, it was necessary to close off the machine: to select some functions and present them in easily recognizable form is necessarily to narrow the user's range of choices.

A key function of middleware is to serve as a software layer that connects the game program (its objects, environments, etc.) to the various machine-specific operating system programs, which govern the behaviour of different computational hardware. Middleware also specifies a programming environment for game creation. It contributes to rationalizing game production by presenting designers with what is effectively a library of choices concerning the dynamic properties of their game. De Prato et al. (2010) summarize the benefits of game engine technology to producers as reducing costs, improving efficiency and effectiveness in the development process, and facilitating the development of cross-platform applications (2010: 68). For example, SDKs make de-bugging and patching more efficient because a repair to one instance of a programmed module is automatically, as it were, a repair to each of its occurrences. Game engines are, as the name implies, the power behind the numerous routines that are familiar from diverse modern games. As De Prato et al. put it:

> The game engine is meant to be in charge of heavy and repeatedly accessed routines, e.g. it deals with graphics rendering and with the 'intelligence' of the game. The engine is in charge of detecting the interaction of entities in the game, the reactions to each action, and so on. Moreover, the middleware provides the developers with an effective development environment. (De Prato et al. 2010: 68)

Once a game engine has been developed and used to power a successful game, it will tend to be used by other designers as well. For example, Renderware, made by Criterion Games in 1993, was originally used to make sports simulators. From 2002 it was used by Rock Star in their *Grand Theft Auto* games and has since been used to make several other games like *Mortal Kombat Armageddon* (2006). Other engines, such as Unreal, cryEngine, Torque and Source, are well known in the industry and some are renowned for handling certain types of feature particularly well – the Havok engine handles vehicle dynamics, for example, while Speed Tree is praised for the way it renders foliage (Nieborg and van der Graaf 2008: 183).

Middleware is expensive and it makes the process of manufacturing games more capital-intensive. As Izushi and Aoyama point out, from the mid-1990s 'video game software development increasingly required capital and a team of developers' (2006: 1853) and this impacted significantly on how the industry was organized. The technology contributes to three related processes, familiar to sociologists who have studied the introduction of technology to other workplaces that formerly had a craft ethos. First, it results in a significant narrowing of options from the point of view of imaginative game design. Programmers are obliged to use the files provided in the SDK and this has a, perhaps imperceptible, effect of inhibiting their own ideas about the directions a game might go in, the kinds of event it might include, even its central concept. Secondly, SDKs rationalize the labour process itself, making it open to more intense specialization while at the same time reducing the necessary skills of each individual worker. Members of a team can be asked to work on particular aspects of a game, specified by components within the SDK, and they do not need to know the bigger picture regarding the overall game, or even the scene they are working on. The negative consequences for workers of this de-skilling are increased because tools like middleware libraries are located in digital space, which means that once the requirements of a given piece of work have been sufficiently well determined, it can be outsourced to a different geographical location where workers are cheaper and perhaps more compliant (Deuze 2007: 342).

The usual route for independent development studios to acquire game engine technology is through the contracts they establish with publishers, who provide access to the technology as part of their commitment to the up-front costs of game development. Increasingly, publishers provide the capital required for game development and it should be acknowledged that, even despite the profitability of the industry as a whole, this is a risky enterprise. Break-even sales points vary by platform, but for console games the average sales target is approximately half a million (Johns 2006: 165; Kerr 2006: 85). Aphra Kerr claims that only about 3 per cent of games are actually profitable (Kerr 2006: 45), while Aoyama and Izushi point out that 14 per cent of games account for 70 per cent of total sales volume (2003: 432), which highlights the dependency of the industry as a whole on a few big sellers – the kinds of games that have become iconic in the culture tend to carry the rest of the industry. Deuze et al. sum up their description of the industry by saying that it has a 'distinct hourglass structure, with a few corporate hardware manufacturers (Microsoft, Sony, Nintendo) and multinational publishers (such as EA, THQ, Activision, UbiSoft and Konami) at one end, and a diverse network of thousands of small studios and service agencies at the other – and very few mid-sized companies in between' (2007: 342). In order to gain access to consoles, developers may be obliged to produce games identified by publishers as 'safe' sellers. This leads to increased standardization of game products, so that more games are produced on time and within budget, but often with fewer interesting features and original ideas. It is largely down to the considerable influence of publishers that 'most, if not all, releases are sequels, franchise titles or film adaptations, rather than unique games' (Deuze et al. 2007: 337). As global media corporations, publishers are cautious about getting involved in controversies that might harm their brand image. Equally, however, when it comes to games, they know that some controversy is needed, especially when it comes to games with a new concept.

The sources of creativity and invention in the games industry tend to be located in independent development studios, which are becoming less numerous as more games production is located in-house, that is, within the console manufacturers or the publishers themselves. Independents are free to make more controversial titles and if, as in the case of Rock Star games, they succeed in making a hit, they can themselves become global corporations. Thereafter, they will tread a similar line between appealing to gamers and lapsing into formulaic or safe products. In-house developers have a number of advantages over independents, including privileged access to new console specifications and middleware, which gives them the edge in terms of technical aspects of game design.

People who work in the games industry are, invariably, invested in gaming as a cultural practice in the sense discussed in the previous chapter: games are made by gamers, with all that that implies (Dovey and Kennedy 2006). The prestige of being involved in game production means that many who work in the industry are prepared to work long hours, sometimes unpaid, and to put up with precarious terms of employment, with one study finding that 36 per cent of workers had put in 65–80 hours in a single week during 'crunch' periods (Deuze et al. 2007: 341). This is despite the fact that the pressure within the industry for cost-cutting and out-sourcing also obliges them to create more standardized products with diminishing original content. In this way, work in the gaming industry exemplifies those features of the 'streamlined worker' discussed in chapter 1. The lines between work and leisure are blurred so that people care about their work and its product for reasons that go beyond their remuneration or their professional status. Short-term project-based work is common, and working life in the games industry is something of an 'adventure'. At the same time, workers often come to realize that their collective investment in, even love of, games and gaming, places them at a disadvantage when it comes to negotiating terms and conditions. This lends a cynical cast to their continued engagement, resulting in gestural protests like the famous 'Easter eggs' that programmers sometimes place inside games programs without their employer's knowledge.[6]

Although middleware has been integral to the organization of games production, it is important to remember that it has itself been shaped by the social context. Improved computer technology, in the sense of machines with larger memories and a greater capacity for processing visual data, indeed, the development of software libraries that expedite specific operations, are all the outcomes of social choices. Most often these reflect the interests of contemporary corporate management, and the same improvements to technical capacity could be used differently. As Saskia Sassen points out, technology use 'is constructed or constituted in terms of specific cultures and practices' (2006: 347), so that 'power, contestation, inequality and hierarchy inscribe electronic space and shape the criteria for what kinds of software get developed' (Sassen 2006: 341).

The context that has shaped contemporary game production and its technologies is the globalization of the industry.

2. Globalization and the Cultures of Production

As Manuel Castells puts it, technology was essential to the creation of 'an economy with the capacity to work as a unit in real time on a planetary scale' (Castells 1996: 92). The internet made it possible for corporations to cast off a geographical centre to their operations because many of their processes could be relocated to digital space, meaning that their geographic location is increasingly notional. The networks that underlie globalization have their origins in the activities of a generation of computer 'whizz kids' who came to maturity in the 1980s (Sassen 2006: 363), many of them having spent their childhoods playing games on Commodore or Spectrum computers. Like the computer game industry, the key global networks were initially formed around a fateful 'triangle of wealth, power and technology' (Castells 1996: 163) in Japan, the US and the EU.[7] Although it is a global industry, in a sense to be explicated below, computer game sales remain quite concentrated in these three centres, with European sales growing in the last decade to become the largest of the three.[8] Other markets are growing rapidly, especially in China, Korea and Vietnam. While games are sold around the world and are often held to be exemplary of a uniform (because technological) global commodity, different hardware platforms are still preferred in different locations.[9]

The computer game industry is an exemplary global business in that its dominant organizations share a strategic orientation which exceeds any particular territorial affiliation. The emergence of globalized businesses did not occur as the result of a simple expansion process in which firms outgrew their national territories. Globalization is not only about a change in scale, but represents a fundamental tipping point reached in the mid-1990s, after which a novel set of cultural 'logics' get inserted into organizations as they encounter new 'strategic geographies of power' (Sassen 2006: 315; Latham and Sassen 2005). The primary focus of a globalized organization is on reaching markets everywhere with products that have been sourced and manufactured in ways that exploit the mobility and reach facilitated by informational networks. For example, Microsoft's X-Box 360 is made in Mexico, Hungary and China (Dyer-Witheford and de Peuter 2009: 76–7; Lugo et al. 2002), while Nintendo and Sony favour locations in Thailand and Brazil (Johns 2006; Kerr 2006).

An illustrative example of the kinds of change involved to the organization of game production by globalization is provided by the publisher and developer, Square (Consalvo 2006; De Prato et al. 2010). Originally founded in Japan in 1985, Square was one of hundreds of developers that made games for the Japanese market, including the *Final Fantasy* games for Nintendo's Famicom[10] console (Consalvo 2006: 126). During the 1990s, Square focused on the Japanese market and its games for the Famicom did not make it to the US or Europe. In 2001, though, Sony bought a significant stake in the company as part of its struggle to ensure a sufficient supply of games for the PS2. In 2003, Square merged with another Japanese developer, Enix, to become Square Enix, while at around the same time they formed connections with the American publisher, EA. In 2003 they combined to form two merged companies, Square Electronic Arts for the US, and Electronic Arts Square for the Japanese market. That alliance concluded with a further merger, resulting in 'Square Enix USA', which by 2008–9 was the eighth-largest publisher in the world, incorporating firms in nearly every continent, including Eidos in London (who published games like *Tomb Raider* (1996), *Deus Ex* (2000) and *Championship Manager* (1992)). The firm has sales and marketing offices strategically located in global cities around the world and owns a global network of development studios, including *Crystal Dynamics* in San Francisco and *IO Interactive* in Denmark. Its revenues for 2009–10 were €250 million (De Prato et al. 2010: 41).

Similar stories can be told about the global integration of firms that started out as small game designers, exclusively focused on local markets. Garry Crawford (2006) has described how the *Championship Manager* series of games began life as a 'bedroom coder' project of brothers Paul and Oliver Collyer. The game was programmed in 1985 on a BBC Micro and seems to have been a hobby:

> The game was eventually picked up by publishers Domark, and the first installment of the *Championship Manager* series (a name the company already owned) was launched in 1992 on Amiga and Atari ST formats. The game had some limited success, which increased with the publication of *CM2* on the PC in 1994, but secured its position as a 'mainstream phenomenon' with the release of *CM3*, which sold more than 55,000 copies in its first week in 2001 . . . By the release of *CM4* in 2003, the *Championship Manager* series had cemented its position as one of the most successful and talked about computer games of all time. (Crawford 2006: 498)

The game was published for a while by Eidos and is now produced in multiple languages for global distribution. It features teams and players from every part of the world where football is played. Like most games, it forms part of the repertoire of products in the sales armoury of a corporation that has no territorial centre. These transformations represent the emergence of gaming as a global phenomenon, but they should not lead us to overlook local variations and the enduring importance of a gaming culture endowed with relatively autonomous criteria of taste.

Notwithstanding this discussion, the new global orientation never succeeds in separating firms entirely from the local contexts and cultures in which they operate. Although computer games were among the first truly global products (Dyer-Witheford and Sharman 2005: 190), games continue to bear the taint of local cultural influence, perhaps reflecting the relatively peripheral status of many smaller developers in relation to global networks and the fact that corporate publishers themselves are aware that gaming tastes continue to vary by geographical region (Consalvo 2006: 192; Ming Kow and Nardi 2009). The digital space in which they operate is not purely technological but simultaneously embedded in 'specific cultures and practices' (Sassen 2006: 347), and gaming's development as a global culture industry involves the entwinement of local factors specific to each of the three points of origin of the industry with technologies that were differently shaped in each of those environments. As we saw in chapter 3, the UK industry grew out of the homebrew subculture centred on home computers, the existence of which accounts for the subsequent prominence of the UK in the global industry (cf. Scheff 1993: 172). Japanese dominance of game and console manufacture from the mid-1980s until the mid-1990s is also explained by a specific convergence of cultural and technological factors.

According to Izushi and Aoyama, the Japanese industry was particularly strong during the period of the US collapse, mainly because it was uniquely well placed to recruit talent from other, neighbouring cultural fields. In particular, there was a strong compatibility of manga art and computer game technology at the time. Nintendo's 8-bit machines provided rapidly moving but not particularly detailed visual content, which was perfect for rendering cartoon art.[11] Japanese developers were able to capitalize on this because both high technology and manga art were esteemed practices in Japanese society. There was no stigma associated with moving between them, but rather a robust cultural bridge, making such personal trajectories plausible and even appealing.[12] They write:

> [T]he creation of industry-specific skills is a complex process which juxtaposes social and economic forces. Before an industry becomes a recognized sector of activities, the necessary skills identified, and a formalized job description

developed, its attraction of labour force relies on a variety of social networks, such as hobby clubs, meetings at shops, trade shows and conventions, alumni of ground-breaking firms in existing industries, and the contacts of an emerging industry's pioneering entrepreneurs. Although economic incentives such as high wages and growth prospects undoubtedly play a role, social acceptance and the legitimacy of an emerging industry and existing industries with potentially relevant skills, as well as the sociocultural cohesiveness between them, facilitate the transfer of skills, affecting entrepreneurial motivation and skills aspirations. (Izushi and Aoyama 2006: 1846)

The most famous person to cross the cultural bridge that existed between the culture of comic book art and technology in Japan was Shigeru Miyamoto, who started his career as a manga artist. In contrast, in the US, comic books have been treated as a low-status art-form and sales have been in decline since the 1940s (Jones 2004). Game developers looking to make successful products were perhaps unlikely to look in that direction for talent. In the UK, comics are viewed as contemptibly childish, while Izushi and Aoyama describe the British film industry of the 1980s as 'elitist', with the consequence that there were few crossovers between any of these fields.[13] The unique convergence of technological capabilities and accessible inputs from elsewhere in the culture made for a strong, creative games industry in Japan.

This argument highlights the entwinement of technology and cultural setting in the development of gaming and the games industry. Game creation is only possible on the basis of a combination of the talents and energies of computing with culturally sanctioned fields of practice with their own values. The case of Miyamoto confirms that this is more than speculation. Something similar happened in Belgium, where there is a culture of esteem for comic book art comparable to that of Japan (Mouchart 2003) and where there have also been significant exchanges. For example, the creator of the *Syberia* (2002, 2004) PC games, Benoit Sokal, was a recognized author of graphic novels before he designed games. The entwinement of technology, markets and developed fields of cultural practice shapes the development of the games industry in each geographical locale. In Latin America, for example, Lugo et al. (2002) describe a situation where development of a games industry was thwarted as recently as the late 1990s, despite the availability of technology and capital, seemingly because relevant actors simply could not perceive producing games as a commercially viable proposition. This is an instance where the requisite cultural perceptions were not in place, despite the availability of capital and technology.

According to Izushi and Aoyama, the new standards of visual computing that arose in the 1990s 'gradually eroded' the advantages of the Japanese industry (Izushi and Aoyama 2006: 1859). They attach particular significance to the '16-bit revolution' pioneered by Sega. As computing generally took a more visual turn (partly inspired by games), so a new generation of consoles changed games into more overtly visual media. They argue that 'a realistic graphic representation became an important marketing tool as both consumers and developers began to judge the quality of games on it' (2006: 1857). The enhanced role for such marketing created a more homogeneous global playing field for games companies, who now competed to produce the most appealing iconic game characters.

As we saw in chapter 3, however, graphics were always a part of game evaluation, even if their quality came to be indexical for something different as gaming acquired more autonomy. Gaming discourse in the 1990s used reference to processor power as indexical not on the resolution or quality of game imagery but rather on gameplay as currently esteemed within the gaming community. This includes references to visual aspects of games, especially the speed with which on-screen imagery moves, but what that signifies is the gaming community articulating its tastes and concerns in an ongoing dialogue with game and console manufacturers.

Izushi and Aoyama maintain technical determinism on this point (2006: 1855), but I think we have to look less at the machines bought by players and focus more on production-side technology to explain the changes of the mid-1990s. As late as 1987, Nintendo had 80 per cent of the US market (Kline et al. 2003: 111), and the heavily capitalized US industry seemed to be reliant on marketing to gain a foothold. In this context, it is surely not irrelevant that the first game engines were produced in the US and the UK in the early 1990s and that they introduced significant economies into the game production process. The technology changes that displaced Japanese games at this time were not entirely to do with the changed visual capacities of gaming consoles, but also reflect the impact of middleware, which enabled the production of games of consistent quality in US and British studios that were compatible with all the available platforms.[14] This high-lights the fact that while technology is an important shaping influence on the development of gaming as a cultural practice, its development and how it gets used to produce games are strongly determined by the strategic concerns of powerful organizations.

From the late 1990s onwards, games were increasingly aimed at global markets, reflecting the fact that computers and consoles had spread to every continent. However, a specific anomaly in the idea that the game industry has become completely detached from local cultures, or, as Mia Consalvo puts it, 'is now unmoored from national borders and cultures and has become its own sphere of influence, defining its own technoregion' (2006: 133), lies in the continuing asymmetry of Japanese and US game sales in their respective 'national' markets. It remains the case that Japanese games sell much better in the US than vice versa. A cursory survey of game charts shows that around 70 per cent of top-selling games in Japan are made by Japanese developers, while in the US, game charts routinely contain at least 50 per cent Japanese games, sometimes more. This leads Consalvo to argue that the hybridization of games is such that the industry cannot be seen as in any sense a manifestation of US cultural dominance. In fact, she points out, there seems to be a flow of cultural products and of power running from East to West, so that 'even as Japanese games successfully travel West, western products have a more difficult time making the round trip' (Consalvo 2006: 125). She invokes the cliché that 'the Japanese market remains somewhat insular' (2006: 138) to explain the disparity. However, her explanation overlooks historically contingent but continuing differences in the organization and culture of national games industries, which might be considered likely to affect the quality of their products and the choices of the people who buy them.

Despite the pressures to standardize discussed above, there is a wealth of anecdotal evidence that relevant differences persist between globalized firms with different national origins and that these differences may have an effect on the character and quality of the final product. Viewed in this way, gamers' preferences, articulated in terms of the quality of gameplay, may be exerting some influence. As Jennifer Johns writes:

> [T]he demands of video game consumers are not homogenizing, as cultural differences remain important considerations for publishers and developers . . . video games, despite their high-technology image, are cultural goods that are read in specific ways depending upon the locality in which they are produced. (Johns 2006: 173)

Johns cites an interviewee who says that Microsoft impose more controls on content than the other console manufacturers (2006: 168), while another says that Sony do not interfere in this way (2006: 170). Johns also points out that the Japanese industry is more firmly located in the Japanese locale.[15] Perhaps most important of all, however, may be the superior integration of the Japanese production process. Pointing out that Japanese console manufacturers prefer to maintain close relationships with a select group of diverse publishers (2003: 432), Aoyama and Izushi write that:

> The co-existence of hardware and software businesses creates a degree of synergy that is deemed critical . . . For instance, at Nintendo's software development division, all staff members, including designers and artists as well as software programmers, are given training in hardware architecture. Shigeru Miyamoto, director of the division, argues that a combination of knowledge about hardware and software allows systematic development of games at all levels within his team. (Aoyama and Izushi 2003: 432)

They go on to report that Miyamoto prefers working with British publishers to US ones because, in his view, 'UK publishers pay attention to the structure of games at all stages of the development process'. This indicates that national industries where aspects of a craft ethos persist, in which workers are able to retain a clear vision of the final product and allow it to inform their, albeit increasingly specialized, activities, make for a superior final product, in the eyes and hands of gamers. As Aoyama and Izushi put it, such an approach is 'based on a solid understanding of hardware architecture, widely shared by Japanese software publishers but seldom found among US publishers' (2003: 435). Similarly, Aphra Kerr reports that Japanese game development teams are smaller and have more content design personnel than their Western counterparts, which makes for a more integrated approach to game production[16] (Kerr 2006: 87), and she goes on to claim that workers enjoy shorter hours and stay in post longer (Kerr 2006: 92). This all points to the enduring importance of local variations in employment and working practices, which are likely to be part of the explanation for the success of Japanese games on global markets. It also highlights the importance of recognizing the active role played by gamers and gaming preferences. These tend to be obscured by scholars who either reduce them to one technologically determined feature of games (the graphics), or exaggerate their manipulated character by explaining the success of games purely by reference to advertising budgets.

3. Technology, Power and Resistance

In the mid-1990s cyberspace was illuminated for the first time. Games made this possible, both in the sense that they were the first applications designed to be colourful and accessible and in that they promoted these things as values. In this sense, games carried the artistic critique discussed in chapter 1 into technology design. Computers spoke to each other in the dark (Sterling 1992) but games, in particular *Myst* and *Doom*, both of which circulated widely in the key year of 1994, brought the darkness to life (Kushner 2003). The idea that computers should be made easy to use by deploying visual metaphors on the human–machine interface, which became part of the common sense of technology design in the 1990s, was pioneered by games like the ones discussed in the previous chapter. The impact of these games was to make the digital space, into which capital was relocating, exciting and attractive. People used the first graphically enabled web-based browsers to download games onto their new PCs. Recapitulating the activity of a previous generation of home computer users, games were commonly the first thing most people did with their newly networked PCs (Wellman and Heythornthwaite 2002: 24), more popular as a 'first use' even than e-mail, and surely more important in promoting the idea that using computers could be 'fun'.

At the same time, games were changed by the encounter with visual computing. As noted above, some scholars have attributed the success of the Playstation, also launched in 1994, to the superior visual capacities of the machine and to the prominence and appeal of iconic game characters. The promotion of these visual representations articulates games and gaming to advertising, which historically has exploited the power of the visual image to suspend rational deliberation and tap into and stimulate the desires of the consumer (Marcuse 1964: 32). This aspect of marketing has been central to the rise of brands in the era of networked capitalism. Here, too, games have had a significant impact, profoundly altering the shape of the contemporary commodity and the dynamics of its consumption.

Lash and Lury identify the mid-1990s as the period when technological incarnations of 'brands' transformed our collective experience of socio-cultural space (Lash and Lury 2007: 43–4). Media objects in particular are no longer meaningful representations to be interpreted by audiences, but objects to be navigated by individuals (Lash and Lury 2007: 9). The new commodities of the global culture industry have a distinctive 'vital' character: as virtuals they seem to possess a kind of life, which leads Lash and Lury to present their study of the new commodity form as a 'humanism of the non-human', aligned to the fashionable idea of an ethnography of things (cf. Appadurai 1988; Latour 2005). Icons play an important role in this, since potent visual images are literally emblematic for social meanings. In acquiring them we import signs into ourselves, with implications for self-comprehension and for how we position ourselves in the meaning-making activities of others. Here, the global culture industry intersects and informs subjective identity formation.

The penetration of commodity consumption and its associated risk of dependency into the deepest recesses of subjective existence is perhaps particularly troubling if we consider marketing to children. Kline et al. (2003) discuss Nintendo's and Sega's use of Mario and Sonic, respectively, as key elements in aggressive marketing strategies when the two competed for dominance in the late 1980s. These campaigns were perceived as insidious because they used the appeal of cartoon characters to children to inveigle their way into parents' wallets, but also because they projected the dubious values associated with gaming into what had been perceived as the 'innocent' play of children. A number of scholars (Crewe and

Collins 2006; Ruckenstein 2010; Hill 2011) have expressed concern that children are increasingly exposed to marketing of games and entertainment commodities. This is worrisome because children have not acquired the robust identities and psychological reserves to withstand a barrage of messages aimed at persuading them to buy things, especially if those things are related to identity and standing in the eyes of their peers. Jennifer Hill also observes a correlation between various negative psychological symptoms and the degree of involvement an individual has in consumer culture, writing that 'children who are more involved in consumer culture are more depressed, more anxious, have lower self-esteem and suffer from more psychosomatic complaints' (Hill 2011: 359). From this she infers that 'psychologically healthy children will be made worse off if they engage in consumer culture' (2011: 359). The inference is not entirely valid, however, since it overlooks the possibility that the causality runs the opposite way to the one she assumes: it is as likely that today's damaged individuals are drawn to consumption as a compensatory behaviour for the various other ways in which their childhood life falls short. Contemporary childhood unhappiness is not necessarily attributable to rampant consumerism, then, but dependency on commodities may be symptomatic of wider changes in the culture. Hill argues that the emergence of digital technologies in the 1980s was a key turning point and lists DVD players, computers, iPods, cell phones and Game Boys as spearheading the corruption of childhood since that time (2011: 359). However, this alignment of technology with the commodity has been a bugbear of critical social thought at least since the 1950s and, as I have argued elsewhere (Kirkpatrick 2008), it is largely unhelpful in the digital era. The incorporation of devices by consumers is both the sign of a real malaise and recuperative.

Other studies, allied to the 'new sociology of childhood' (Matthews 2007), indicate that the rise of digital technologies is actually empowering for children in perhaps surprising ways. Since the advent of home computing, children have been allowed to step into the role of resident technology expert in many homes, for example (Aarsand 2007; Aarsand and Aronsson 2009). Parents and grandparents position children as authoritative and allow them to guide choices about which new camera or DVD player to buy, but also how to get the most out of it once it has been acquired. Childhood is not a pure state to be protected from 'new' technologies. Neither is it simply the phase of life in which we are prepared for 'real' adult roles. As Sarah Matthews (2007) points out, children have agency: they contribute to the making and shaping of culture in the present. We can see evidence for this in connection with game icons too. Kline et al. (2003) allege that Sony's character *Crash Bandicoot* was conceived primarily as a marketing response to Mario and Sonic. However, it is simply implausible to claim that Crash Bandicoot is a case of 'advertising preceding play' (2003: 154), as anyone who has played the games will be in a position to confirm. Crash Bandicoot feels completely different from any of the other games, and controlling Crash (or any of his friends) in a round of *Crash Bash* (2000) involves unique sensations appreciated by gamers as excellent gameplay. It is clear that as well as being manipulated by game and advertising imagery, gamers are also equipped by gaming culture to push back, deploying gaming discourse as a resource. This is by no means always a 'wholesome' thing to behold. Sega's *Mortal Kombat* (1992), for example, enabled them to compete with Nintendo because ripping out your opponent's spine appealed to gamer tastes (Kline et al. 2003: 136).[17]

Viewed in this perspective, technology is very much the chink in contemporary capitalism's armour. Commodities and advertising may enter our homes and schools, but as long as they retain their technical character there will always be openings for imaginative interventions and subversive play. The active role played by children and young people in hacking, modding and reconfiguring commodified technology is an important part of contemporary technical politics, in which rival constituencies vie for control over design decisions (Feenberg 2002; 2010). Its effects have been most dramatic in recent years in connection with the music industry (David 2010), where corporations have largely lost control over musical creativity, and the culture of sharing and downloading has created many more spaces for new music and musicians to flourish without having to participate in their own exploitation or that of their audiences.

The use of technology to enforce proprietary claims, especially in relation to intellectual property, is now a well-established part of the digital economy and, as seen above, it was a method pioneered by Nintendo in the late 1980s (Scheff 1993: 236). The original digital networks that have given rise to the information society were predominantly public, and their use by private commercial and corporate interests can be seen as a kind of appropriation of public goods. This was certainly the perspective of many in the hacker movement of the 1980s and 1990s (Levy 1984; Taylor 1999). From their perspective, the attempt to impose restrictions on movement within digital spaces was unjustifiable. The first international hacker conference took place in 1984. Fred Turner (2006: 132–3) describes how hackers became 'self-aware' at this time and started referring to themselves as 'hackers', drawing on Steven Levy's study in much the same way that gamers were drawing on magazines and other materials to constitute themselves as a community at the same time. The hacker ethic maintained that information should be free and available to all. If information was to be restricted, then it was the responsibility of the owner not to put it in a place hackers could find it, that is, a machine connected to the internet.

The 1990s computer culture was divided along these lines, with advocates of a 'hacker aesthetic' facing off against the spread of a kind of computing that encouraged people to relate to their machines as 'users', through the medium of easy-to-use interfaces with intuitive controls. The user here

shades very easily into the 'consumer' who is guided to seductive retail web-sites rather than having to think in technical
terms. This was the context in which hacking was demonized
and ultimately criminalized (Chandler 1996). Game players
who also want to reprogram or modify ('mod') commercially
produced games face an ostensibly similar position to that of
other hackers. The activity has an unbroken history, dating
back to the bedroom coders of the 1980s. It includes the practice of 'chipping' X-Boxes, which became popular in 2002–3,
to make them accessible to Sony and Nintendo games, and
more recently Nintendo devices have been chippable using
the 'Wiikey' chip that allows people to play games on the Wii
that are either from outside their machine's zone or are
pirated in the sense that they have been copied onto DVD-Rs.
Dyer-Witheford and de Peuter report that players have even
taken control of X-Box live game services by hacking the
servers that host the games (Dyer-Witheford and de Peuter
2009: 91). These activities can be seen as an extension of
hacking and as a challenge to the hold of commercial interests
over digital space, in this case the spaces of game play.

However, the social and cultural construction of game
modding has been much less disciplinary in its tone and
content than the discourse around hacking, which has largely
succeeded in establishing the distinction of legitimate from
illegitimate computing practice and in codifying the distinction in law. Modding has not been demonized in the same
way as other kinds of hacking, even by games corporations,
and has rarely been described as a 'crime' in the mainstream
press. Rather than attempt to establish a discourse that disci-
plines and sorts, the games industry has developed strategies
of inclusion to incorporate the energies of modders as a
source of value in the games economy. This is evident from
the wording of end user licence agreements (EULAs), which
rarely involve strict prohibitions on users tinkering with
source code. In fact, source code and level editors are often
made available with games in a kind of invitation to gamers

to design their own add-ons for games and to customize them.[18] In this sense, modding is not only encouraged by the games industry but has secured quite high-profile recognition, with a number of competitions each year, sponsored by industry bodies, and carrying large prizes such as the 'Make Something to Feel' contest, which has a million dollar prize, and the annual Game Developers Conference mod competition (Deuze et al. 2007: 346). These events continue the tradition within gaming of competitions for new, young designers, which were a strong feature of the bedroom coder culture that prevailed in the UK in the 1980s.

By taking a different strategic approach, the games industry aims to incorporate players and channel their creative energies, rather than attempting to impose proprietorial controls. José van Dijck (2009) argues the labour of modding is actually productive of value for media corporations. The terms of most EULAs establish that ownership of modified product remains with the game publisher.[19] Mods extend the shelf life of games that would otherwise be nearing the end of their marketability. The fact that the work of content-creation seems like play is also significant, not for its emancipatory implications, but because it contributes to the pressures on workers employed in the industry, discussed above. 'Mixed models' (van Dijck 2009: 50) of labour, involving amateurs like modders and designer developers who were themselves enthusiasts and hobbyists only a short time before being employed in the industry contributes to the pressure on the latter to be more productive and drives down their wages and conditions. Viewed in this way, the recuperative effects of activities like modding are also the route to further exploitation. From the perspective of the games industry, modding is free labour that prolongs the life of media commodities, introducing the kind of superficial changes that stimulate extra interest in games that would otherwise be coming to the end of their shelf lives. Van Dijck concludes that, in fact, 'user agency is defined more than ever by the capital-intensive and technology-driven economies of global, vertically integrated markets' (van Dijck 2009: 54).

Although modding is not limited in principle in its scope, the 'total conversion mod' that effects a profound transformation of the game engine, like the famous conversion of *Half-Life* (1998) from a single-player game to the multi-player *Counter-strike* (1999), is now extremely rare (Nieborg and van der Graaf 2008: 187), for reasons described above. Modders' access is always restricted in practice partly by the sheer scale of contemporary games. The 'key organizing role of the game engine' (Nieborg and van der Graaf 2008: 179) applies to modders and developers alike. Modding, then, cannot revive the enterprise and creativity of the bedroom coder generation nor the hacktivism of the 1990s. Rather, it is co-opted labour and the dominant role of engine technologies means that for the most part its products will be conservative and superficial: 'Whatever the scale and scope of a mod, it will always function within the original game's proprietary structure' (Nieborg and van der Graaf 2008: 184). From this perspective, mods are simply extensions of existing products and no kind of challenge to the existing regime of digital property.

However, modding does involve players expressing themselves by creating new content. It involves creative activity ennobled and empowered by mastery of an expressive medium whose logic is not subordinate to the needs of industrial production or instrumental reason, paradigmatic for the kind of resistance art offered to the traditional culture industry. This activity resembles what Adorno (2002) called autonomous aesthetic technique' and would seem to be the very opposite of passive consumption. Engaging with game objects in non-prescribed (if not actually proscribed) ways involves much more than merely consuming someone else's off-the-shelf product. Mods are shared within the on-line gaming community and can be esteemed for their gameplay, while others are designed and used as training programs gamers use to improve skills in particular sequences of play (Prax 2012). Modding is a refusal by gamers of limitations on their access to knowledge and understanding. If the traditional entertainment commodity involves the fetishistic sheen of technological power, modding can be seen as the human element working its way back in.

The most famous mods do not inspire critical theorists with their emancipatory potential. The 'hot coffee' mod of *Grand Theft Auto: San Andreas* (2006), for instance, involves pornographic scenes that Dyer-Witheford and de Peuter (2009) interpret as reinforcing racial stereotypes. What we see here is not the resistance of a socialist or counter-cultural *avant garde*. Its interest lies less at the level of its content (which is cheeky, cynical and gestural – as we should expect) but in what it tells us about the social imaginary. Gamers esteem good games and game modding is an attempt to create objects that appeal within the imagined gaming community. It is true that we are more entangled in our objects than ever and each of them constitutes a 'micro-structure of power', a script which choreographs our actions (Lash and Lury 2007). What modding shows is that gamers sometimes write their own scripts. This activity is always powerfully configured by the underlying technological form of the game commodity and its value is often extracted to serve the ends of the system, but we should not be misled by this into thinking that the recuperative element of play and gaming is merely functional for the reproduction of networked capitalism. A more measured judgement would be that people still engage in creative play and the values associated with this activity continue to connect them to an imagined community, in which gameplay is the central operative value. The culture in which the idea of a good game is reflected on and examples are appraised, discussed and performed exerts real effects. These can be seen in popular rejection of boring games and in the demand for shocking titles as well as in game modding, which, although it is a constrained form of creativity, is nonetheless a point at which the system occasionally loses its grip. The demand for, and sometimes even creation of, superior gameplay is a value that, in its cheeky ambiguity and amorphous indecipherability, continues to gnaw away at the plans of the commercial giants.

CHAPTER FIVE

The Phenakisticon

The previous two chapters have suggested that computer games are recuperative for individuals and that a perverse consequence of their effectiveness in this is sometimes the extension of aspects of the system that make recuperation necessary. However, this analysis has largely overlooked the way that computer gaming not only offers scope for individual play and imagined community with other gamers, but also has acquired a very concrete, social dimension. Massive multi-player on-line games (MMPGs), in particular, involve people playing together in game worlds, establishing relationships and working together on freely chosen ludic projects. This kind of activity suggests there may be something recuperative here that, rather than reinforcing or extending the system, might point beyond it. A new sociality, involving creative social interaction, may add another dimension to the theme of recuperation. As we have seen, recognition of each other's gaming accomplishments, assessed in terms of the quality of their gameplay, is central to gamer culture. The develop-ment of a normative context in which great gameplay is esteemed, from high scores on arcade machines to organized competitions and professional tournaments (Taylor 2012), has been essential to the development of gaming as a cultural practice. In MMPGs, this aspect of recognition for one's achievements becomes important to progress in the game and in this way esteem for gameplay is inscribed in an ongoing set of interpersonal relationships. Recuperation here seems to take the form of playful, non-instrumentalized social rela-tionships at the margins of the global culture industry. Such a development might suggest the possibility of authentic sociality, a place where critique might secure a foothold.

The origins of MMPGs can be traced back at least to the 1980s when, as we saw in chapters 2 and 3, people already played adventure games on networked computers. These practices showed how computer gaming always included an important social orientation: people like to play games with other people. The single-player games of the 1980s were something of an aberration in the wider history of ludic formats. In the 1990s, text-based on-line worlds, most famously LambdaMOO, became popular within the computing fraternity, attracting a few thousand players at a time. In the middle of the decade, players created local area networks to play multi-player versions of games like *Doom*, resulting in local area network (LAN) gaming (Jansz and Martens 2005). The first modern MMPG, however, was *Ultima On-line*, which launched in 1997 and at its peak a couple of years later had several hundred thousand regular players. *Ultima* was followed by a succession of other MMPGs, most famously *Ever-Quest* (1999) and recently *World of Warcraft* (2004). Both these games have been through several iterations and re-launches, which involve extensive changes to the environment and to the challenge and reward structures of the games. *World of Warcraft* is the most popular such game and currently (2011) claims over 11 million registered subscribers.

For early commentators, it seemed that these games offered a kind of utopian escape from the real world (Rheingold 1997). Subsequently, theorists have suggested that they might be the point of departure for a revived form of civil society, playing a similar role to eighteenth-century coffee houses by bringing people together under conditions where they can share opinions and formulate visions of political change appropriate to the new, globalized world of informational capitalism. The current chapter draws on recent studies of life in MMPGs to offer a more sceptical view. My argument centres on the kinds of recognition and respect available in

MMPGs. Drawing on ideas from Axel Honneth (1995), especially his notion of civil society as grounded in recognition, I argue that MMPGs cannot constitute a point from which effective critique might spring, but are rather suggestive for the extent to which increased dependency on the global culture industry has eaten into subjective psychological reserves. In keeping with the central theme of the book, I argue that the recuperative gains of MMPG activity are won at the price of extending the reach of corporate interests into our everyday lives and social relationships. This frames critique, limiting it to a kind of cynical gesture at power, rather than a sustained challenge with the potential to surpass the dominant reality.

The chapter begins with an account of Honneth's thesis concerning the importance of recognition and the psychological bases of the struggles for respect that define a healthy polity. It then examines the idea of a personality structure that is consistent with such a struggle and questions whether the requisite conditions for such a subject are present in MMPGs. Here I draw on recent studies that suggest a diversity of player styles and important differences in how people use the games, with implications for what they draw from the experience. Attention then turns in the second section to the way that the rules inscribed in the technologically defined environments of MMPGs encourage specific kinds of social interaction on the part of players. This analysis shows that the sociability of MMPGs is subject to important constraints which are clarified by the recognition-theoretic approach. Here, too, there are important differences between games, and the discussion compares the role of social performance found in *EverQuest* (*EQ*) with that in *World of Warcraft* (*WoW*). This contrast points towards an increased play with recognition itself as the content of game worlds and to a corresponding diminution of gaming norms as operative in the culture of the game.

The final section argues that increasingly what we see in game worlds and other new social media (NSM) is a play with the conditions of authentic sociality that feeds off and contributes to generalized confusion about the real motivations of others. This should not be confused with earlier ideas about the dangers of anonymity in 'cyberspace' environments. In fact, the confused information we exchange in MMPGs is consistent with the fact that we now usually know who our digital interlocutors are. What we do not know is whether they (or indeed we) are sincere; the earnestness of our interaction is always in question. Here, MMPG culture is positioned in the wider context of the contemporary social imaginary. When gameplay loses purchase in the normative assessment of games, we cannot really speak, as some have done, of a 'gamification' or ludification of social interaction. As in NSM, it seems that increasingly we play with sociality itself and with the very idea of a well-grounded meaningful connection to others.[1] In fact, I argue that increasingly empty and inauthentic social relationships motivated by a desire for authentic social connection are driving down on gameness and exploiting it as a source of recuperative values in contemporary culture in a process better described as ludefaction.

1. MMPGs in Recognition-Theoretic Perspective

MMPGs are, as Edward Castronova puts it, 'more than just souped-up computer games' (2005: 22); they are 'synthetic worlds'. What he means by this is that they are places in which people establish connections with others and participate in a range of practices that make these connections meaningful.[2] The relationships people form in on-line environments like MMPGs often feel as important to them as other kinds of relationship forged in more traditional spaces. The close reflexive ties between social connection and personal identity mean that this has implications for how people understand themselves. Sustained interaction with others within a context of recognized and sometimes shared purposes is the kind of experience that will shape who we are. Membership of a game world, therefore, is tantamount to membership of a society. Celia Pearce (2009) describes how players of the *URU: Ages beyond myst* (2003) game world became 'migrants' after that game closed down, moving *en masse* to play in other game worlds. The connection and shared sense of community players felt outlived the technologically defined environment.

Media of the old culture industry were held to impoverish social relations, creating subjects who were more prone to dependency on passive consumption to buttress their identity. As we saw in chapter 4, new media objects seem to make this worse in that they demand active labour from consumers who are then all the more dependent on things to sustain their identities. The new spirit of capitalism demands streamlined individuals who are prepared to pay money and work in return for an increasingly thin return in terms of resources of self-construction and identity maintenance. In this context, recognition from others of one's play and of its value becomes more important than ever. Gaming culture is a recuperative resource in this sense. MMPGs offer the possibility of contact with other gamers in ludic situations. Exploring the value of this raises deeper questions about the self who secures recognition and esteem in such a way. Is it the kind of self that might participate in a society of equal citizens equipped to counter injustice and demand equal rights? Are MMPGs the kinds of social spaces that might promote such individuals? Axel Honneth's (1995) recognition-theoretic approach to social relations is a useful basis, consistent with the approach adopted throughout this book, upon which to address these questions.

At the heart of Honneth's approach is the principle, derived from G.H. Mead (1987 [1934]), that it is through securing recognition from others that individuals learn things about themselves and ultimately discover who they are. At a primary level, this involves being loved as a child, which equips human beings with the ability to recognize and understand their own 'needs and urges' as legitimate (Honneth 1995: 118). A second dimension of recognition concerns self-respect, which people get from living in a society with rules which protect and benefit them as much as they do other citizens. Only when people know that they enjoy the protections of the law can they also feel that they themselves are, potentially at least, its authors. This forms the starting point for feelings of solidarity, which characterize the third dimension of Honneth's approach. Individuals who are sufficiently confident in their own subjective reactions and who possess self-respect will be able to recognize and respond to situations where they perceive unfairness. At this point, they will mount recognition claims, which are aimed at attracting the support of others with similar convictions, and this will form the basis for widening the circle of recognition that underpins a society. The resulting connection is solidarity on Honneth's definition, and a vibrant civil society will involve people acting in solidarity with one another to achieve recognition for themselves or other parties they perceive as being disrespected, or from whom appropriate kinds of recognition are being withheld.

A society of assertive citizens will be one in which people experience formative relationships that allow them to trust their own feelings, needs and urges. This dimension of selfhood and personal development relies upon the presence of loving relationships, which are, paradoxically, formed through a process of separation. Love is a kind of recognition that is afforded to most people by their mothers during early development, but it is secured only when the child starts to lash out and differentiate him- or herself from the parent. During this phase, the infant learns that the parent is independent yet still suffers their attacks, while the parent recognizes the child in its independence and is therefore able to extend proper recognition (love, rather than unity) to them. Of particular importance to this process are the right kinds of transitional objects (Honneth 1995: 104). Toys and other objects that the child identifies with during the separation process should be of a kind that allows them to be creative, but not to indulge in pathological behaviours that might constitute unhealthy obsession, which might derail or stall the process. Honneth refers to Donald Winnicott (1971), who distinguishes between play that unlocks creativity and self-expression on one side and the kind that is consistent with avoiding difficult feelings on the other. It is only on the basis of an individuation process based in love that people can cope with being alone and, most importantly, can experience openness to the inner self or 'I', the source of individual creativity, without anxiety.[3] Self-respect means that you can be an 'I', rather than a 'me', without stirring up fears of abandonment[4] and is also the condition of possibility of real friendships (Honneth 1995: 104).

Studies of MMPGs reveal that social processes susceptible to recognition-theoretic analysis are common, even the very stuff of life, in game worlds. However, using Honneth's theory, we can identify important shortcomings and distorting effects, operative at each of the three levels of love, self-respect and solidarity, which ought to inform our appraisal of the potential of MMPGs to offer a valid alter-sociality, or a platform for critique.

Sherry Turkle's (1995) early internet research describes a tendency for people to fall in love quickly in chat rooms and multi-user domains (MUDs), but also documents the subsequent failure of many, perhaps most, of those relationships. A similar pattern is also evident in MMPGs. According to Yee (2006: 320) 25–30 per cent of players report sharing a confidence they wouldn't share with intimates off-line, and 40–45 per cent say they are more satisfied with on-line than off-line friendships. Yet 21 per cent of guilds in *World of Warcraft* disappear each month (Williams et al. 2006), indicating a certain fragility to these relatively intense in-game social attachments.

The existing literature tends to attribute this effect to limitations on the communications capacities of digital media. Using social network analysis to study new media, Caroline Haythornthwaite (2002) says that multiple, broad channels of communication correlate to stronger, more durable social attachments. Intimate connection seems to be accelerated by the kinds of communication channel that are made available in MMPGs. Instead of seeing a full-bodied individual exuding the full range of implicit and explicit information that appearance and disposition confer upon speech acts in natural contexts, all we have is their speech, or some text, in a context where we are working together with a shared sense of purpose, against a background which inclines us to view the other favourably. Consequently, new media channels tend to promote weak ties that are nonetheless freighted with relatively intense feeling.

Recent research by Williams et al. (2011) also suggests a connection between narrowed communications and increased susceptibility of individuals to group influences on their behaviours. On this interpretation, the fast route to intimacy is enhanced by the fact that much of the spadework of relationship building in other contexts – calling people on the phone, arranging to meet, maintaining concern with events in their lives – is handled in abbreviated form by the game technology. A meeting, for instance, requires little effort in this artificial environment and the range of important events is fairly limited. These kinds of expeditious handling of the labour of relationship maintenance tend to go unnoticed once players get used to them, and their effect is to force the positive benefits of collaboration into clearer view. One result of this is that feelings of trust may be heightened out of proportion to the information people have about one another or the presence of real sentiment (the kind that motivates all the work of relationship building in natural contexts) on either side. This pattern has also been noted in connection with newer social media,[5] with which *WoW* in particular bears a strong affinity – here, as before, computer games have pioneered tendencies in digital technology design. Voice communication channels are particularly useful in certain game situations but the human voice can add to the feeling of personal connection. Williams et al. (2006) report that, aware of the effect described here, some players choose to limit their exposure to this kind of communication.

However, while the communication channels available in games are surely a factor in explaining the kinds of attachment we find there, we also need to ask why people are drawn to communicate in this way in the first place. There is a profound ambivalence associated with play in these games, which needs to be understood in its wider social context. The pattern is one of dependency, which reflects an underlying lack of confidence on the part of most players in the legitimacy of their own needs.

The activity of playing in an MMPG bears the outward appearance of a serious commitment for most players. The average player is in the game for a few hours a day, several times a week, and they attach significance to the experiences they have there, including social experiences. Yee also says that nearly half of MMPG players describe themselves as 'addicted' to the games (2006: 323), which he interprets as a sign of 'emotional investment' and a tribute to the 'tremendous appeal' of the game environment. However, there has been controversy, at least since the 'rape in cyberspace' incident of 1992 (Dibbell 1991), over the extent to which players are actually invested in their characters and take the activities in these game worlds seriously.[6] For some, the temporary loss of control over one's character caused by a malicious hack or a technical fault, for example, seems to be experienced as a trauma, while others view it as a mild irritation akin to that caused by any other gadget not working properly. It seems that players vary in the significance they attach to their in-game connections, with most choosing to shift between playing a role and communicating 'as themselves' with other characters.

The relevant contrast here is between 'normal' players and 'role players' (RPers). Only 5 per cent of MMPG players are serious role players[7] in the sense that they take the fictional role they occupy, as a wood elf or a gangster, so seriously that they only speak and perform actions they think are appropriate to their character when they are playing the game. They can be emphatic about only playing in character, rejecting other people's attempts to communicate 'out of character' as disruptive. RPers tend to play less, for shorter periods, than others, perhaps a few hours a week as against the average 22 hours (Yee 2006). Williams et al. say that RPers 'tend to be slightly younger, have a higher percentage of females and to be slightly less well educated' (2011: 182). They go on to report that 'more RP meant having physical, mental, and clinically diagnosed problems at a far worse rate than their counterparts' (2011: 184). Moreover, RPers are 'more lonely, less happy, more likely to be disabled, and more likely to have been diagnosed with depression, substance addictions, behavioral addictions, attention-deficit disorder, and learning disabilities' (2011: 184). On this portrayal, RPers tend to be 'psychologically burdened' individuals, which means they are more vulnerable and drawn from marginal social groups. These players make a substantial and largely unacknowledged contribution to making games attractive and interesting to other players. They are more likely to identify themselves as troubled by feelings of loneliness.

The obvious reading of this casts RPers as the psychologically problematic group. However, I think it would be a mistake to view RPers as the 'troubled' sector of the gaming public. Rather, their confessed vulnerabilities, along with their in-game contributions, could be read as a sign of greater creativity and should be interpreted as indicating greater openness to the Meadian 'I'. Yee's reference to the high levels of reported addiction amongst supposedly more 'normal' players is not reassuring, as addiction is an illness associated with behaviours most people consider pathological. David Golumbia (2009) argues that the popular understanding of addiction in this context carries the connotation of compulsion and that MMPGs '*demand* intimate and profound engagement from individual users' (Golumbia 2009: 196, emphasis added). It is important to bear in mind that Yee's respondents are using the term in this popular way, in response to a direct question – 'Do you consider yourself addicted?' – amongst other questions about their behaviour in the game and its appeal.[8]

Non-RPers report fewer problems to do with isolation and depression, but they exist in a grey, borderline area as far as the game's ostensible fiction and their role in it are concerned, neither investing in it fully nor repudiating it, which would lead to rejection of the game. They present as ambivalent between playing a role and being one's ordinary self. It seems to me that this must go together with a kind of lack of conviction, even cynicism, about one's own activity, which, given the scale of the temporal investments just discussed, lacks clear historical precedents.[9] The implications of this grow in significance when we consider the kinds of collaboration that occur in MMPGs, but clearly it touches on the question of doubts about one's own status and reflects a willingness to comply, to find the correct rules by acquiescing to what others are doing, while keeping one foot on the other, non-committed side of the fence. Viewed in this way, RPers display greater integrity and, perhaps, suffer the psychological consequences of at least trying to construct an alternative, imagined reality in the game world, while most players do not. More 'normal' players depend on the game in the sense that they do not see the necessity of such experimentation in an environment already saturated in fiction. Moreover, as I will emphasize below, they have no ostensible reason for appearing the way they do in the game world, or for doing the things they do there.

It is quite telling here that all MMPGs involve repetitious, grinding action sequences that are not pleasurable or meaningful in themselves. Grinding refers to a process, like repeatedly hacking at the roots of a tree or fighting the same unchallenging foe over and over again, when there is a clear pay-off from the activity in terms of game goods but little in the way of pleasurable challenge. The prevalence of such sequences has led Golumbia (2009) to deny that MMPGs – he studies WoW – are playful at all. Viewed in terms of Winnicott's (1971) distinction mentioned above, the emphasis on repetitious sequences combined with a focused, aggressive disposition, would only be a pathological form of play. 'Normal' MMPG play is compulsive-addictive and involves repetitious behaviours, especially the practice of grinding, that probably have more to do with keeping the fear of being alone at bay than with allowing the individual to develop his or her creative and expressive powers. So much, then, for the idea that RPers, who play less and 'act' more are psychologically more vulnerable: it is more likely that they differ mainly in knowing how vulnerable they are. The 'normal' MMPG gamer participates on terms that are uncertain, even if it is easy to impute motives (play and social connection) to their activity. This kind of uncertainty reflects a deep ambivalence about the legitimacy of one's own desires – I will be an elf for 22 hours this week but I won't really commit to the role – which precedes and underscores most players' participation in the game and their encounter with its distinctive communication channels.

2. The Limitations of Engineered Sociability

In modern societies, we respect each other as bearers of rights and this is a non-affective yet supposedly determinate form of recognition. The fact that it is detached from any affective, subjectively meaningful tie is definitive for modern law, which applies to all equally. In traditional societies, in contrast, the concept of honour was decisive and applied differently to different categories of person. The key structural difference between the two concerns what Honneth calls an 'essential indeterminacy' in modern societies 'as to what constitutes the status of a responsible person', which leads to 'structural openness' in the law. It is always possible to widen the applicability of the law and to refine its application so that it becomes progressively more inclusive and does so in ways that are meaningful (not too abstract) for everyone, regardless of factors like income.[10]

Intriguingly, MMPGs push back to a traditional variant of respect in which honour is important because what is viewed positively is substantive ethics, manifest in a style of life. In MMPGs, players are offered more than one framework for such a substantive ethics within which to locate themselves and be perceived as valuable by others. Playing as a particular kind or type of character with the appropriate style (and making the 'right' choices) are also manifestations of such a substantive ethics. A good case could be made for viewing MMPGs as environments that afford resources for a positive ethics of selfhood based in such aesthetic considerations of style and performance, along the lines described by the late Foucault in his study of Classical culture (O'Leary 2002). An aesthetics of 'caring for the self', fashioning a subjective identity in light of a concern with how others will perceive it, supplants adherence to ethical codes that apply to all equally.

The new player of a MMPG begins by designing their avatar. In one of the most famous games, *EverQuest* (1999), this involves choosing to be a member of a 'race', of which there are 16 varieties. Within each race, there are further available options, so that a barbarian can be a berserker, for example, or a warrior. These choices position players in the game because each avatar type starts off with a different initial set of points. The combinations of choices also result in avatars that find it easier to do some things in the game than others. For example, in many games 'warriors' are effective fighters but lack other abilities, like healing, that are also important in the course of play, and find it more difficult, if not impossible, to acquire those skills. Player choices at this stage, then, already commit them to a certain set of strategies and limit their ludic and performative dispositions in ways that may not be entirely predictable from the outset.

Beyond the configuration of character in terms of in-game affordances, which are determined by this initial choice, players are also required to design the visual appearance of their avatar. The dress, armour and other visual items that are worn communicate to other players in much the same way that personal appearance communicates in other social con-texts. Female players report dissatisfaction with the available choices, which tend to cast avatars that are gendered female within a limited clothing repertoire (Taylor 2006). When players gain experience in the game and secure achievements, this is signified by their acquisition of further accoutrements, so that questions of taste and of status merge in the course of participation in the game (Klastrup 2009; Taylor 2006). In many games the scrutiny of other characters is a designed-in affordance of the game world, instantiated by the 'look' command or its cognates.

The choice of avatar affects how we are perceived by others in the game, but it also limits the kind of role or function a player's character can take on in the course of particular game sequences. Yee (2009) writes that 'players are able to befriend those who have demonstrated their courage, honour and loyalty' in the game. I may meet you initially as a wood elf but in the course of a raid or a fight I will discover real things about you and these will enable me to form a judgement about you as a person. Similarly, you will gain information about who I am, really, but the understanding we have of each other will be framed by the inherent limitations we have imposed on our actions through our initial choices (to be this type or race rather than that) in the setting-up phase of the game. Moreover, one of the first things we will know about each other is that we came here and half-pretended to be these characters. All of this is significant because it bears upon the kind of recognition we can afford one another and the sort of self-respect we can derive from the activity. The mediation of our relationship through our avatars, with their built-in constraints of type, is not straightforward in diminishing the content of our relationship, but it does distort the kinds of recognition we are able to afford one another. This should be unsettling precisely because the relationships people form in MMPGs can be perceived by them as important.

Referring to contemporary biotechnologies that could be used to shape individuals (their talents, specific abilities) before they are born, Jürgen Habermas writes that 'the dividing line between the nature we *are* and the organic equipment we *give* ourselves is being blurred' (2003: 22). At stake here is 'a prior ethical self-understanding of the species, which is shared by all moral persons' (2003: 40) and which is foundational for the existence of an ethical community. Only on the basis of a sense that I am fundamentally as good as anyone else can I have the self-respect necessary to assert my rights, and other people's, as those of free citizens. If technology blurs the categorical distinction between this fundamental identity and the constitutive differences between individuals, then it constitutes an intrusion that will be corrosive to those relationships in which natural equality is otherwise presupposed (2003: 64). Habermas contrasts such interventions with socialization processes, or the case of parents buying superior education for their children, because technological interventions are irreversible, asymmetric, not communicatively mediated and corrosive to relationships based on respect for the other as an equal. We can see that these conditions also apply in the case of MMPGs: a choice of character type is irrevocable for the duration of an avatar's existence in the game; it means they will always be good at some things and useless at others, and this determines their difference from others with different traits. While the game world is inherently communicative, avatar construction skews communicative interaction. For instance, raiding parties will always want to include at least one cleric for healing purposes but they will rarely want more than a certain number of each avatar type, so players will be excluded from some activities on the basis of how they have been programmed: matching races up to create effective teams is a 'primary concern' when raiding parties, guilds and fellowships are being set up (Bennerstedt and Ivarsson 2010: 212).

What makes this kind of limitation so disturbing – and stirs an intuitive apprehension around biotechnologies, a feeling that something is wrong even though it is difficult to say what it is (Habermas 2003: 16) – is that it touches on people's self-understanding. As Habermas puts it:

> Getting used to having human life biotechnologically at the disposal of our contingent preferences cannot help but change our normative self-understanding. (2003: 72)

Something similar happens when people choose to live part of their lives as avatars, to embrace the idea that they can conduct important social performances through technological media that efface their natural sameness with others. There is, as Tanner Higgin (2009) points out, a disturbing analogy here with racism, which also attempts to assign social roles according to designated biological traits, except that here the different capacities are real because they have been programmed into the situation.

In MMPGs, millions of people have assumed social roles based on modes of activity and self-representation drawn from a menu that includes built-in constraints that can never be overcome by virtuous (or other) effort.[11] This distortion of core recognition processes (ones that are fundamental to self-respect) is most clear in the fact that, as a cleric in WoW, for example, I cannot hope to achieve recognition for my robust skills in combat but only for my healing abilities. Of course, this is only in a game, but in fact, as we will see, real concern hangs over what that means in connection with MMPGs and how successfully the notion of gameness operates to inoculate practices here against the world beyond. I am not suggesting that the avatar is a real, surgically or genetically transformed body, rather that in entering this set of practices and becoming an MMPG player, we are obliged to accept that when we do things with our real bodies (press this key, move the mouse over here), it will necessarily have different consequences than when someone else performs those same actions. Moreover, these differences of outcome will be things that matter to us (although the extent of this is ambiguous) and the limiting differences will be things that we cannot overcome.[12] What we acquire when we make this choice is admission to a world of programmed asymmetries that control social status and recognition. Inevitably this will have implications for how others view us and how we view ourselves.

The extent to which a person is invested in their avatar, viewing it as an extension of their 'real self' as against a counter they manipulate in a game or a role they assume for some kind of dramatic effect, varies according to their style of play – we have seen that RPers are unusual in this regard. It is also affected by the nature of the social experiences people have while playing the game. Securing positive recognition from others for things they have done will encourage a player to view their own action positively and to incorporate that perception into their self-understanding. Some gamers meet each other off-line (Taylor 2006), so that membership of a guild, gang or raiding party is not always the shallow or transient commitment it might seem to be.[13] As Sal Humphreys (2009) points out, the exit costs for players once they have signed up to and begun to participate in a game are in this sense high, so that the decision to become a player cannot be understood like any other purchase of similar monetary value.[14] The main cost she has in mind is precisely the loss of social connection. The sociality formed here is clearly real, but it has an engineered character that ought to inform our assessment of its sociological significance.

The amount of social interaction one experiences in an MMPG tends to grow, from an initial phase of exploration and finding one's way around, during which time one meets occasional others who are helpful – or not. First encounters with other people can be openings onto alliances with them or just brushes without subsequent import. This is followed by an extended second phase, which is commonly marked by attachment to a specific group or groups of other players, interspersed by periods of solo play. Most, perhaps all, MMPGs incentivize the building of contacts and joining groups. There is variation here, however. Simon et al. (2009) argue that the 'grinding' phase, during which players perform repetitious actions to build up their avatar's status and abilities is also a sociable period in *EQ*, but, as David Golumbia (2009) points out, it is a relatively solitary phase for players of *WoW*.

As indicated above, game environments themselves put people in the mood to be receptive, even friendly. This is related to the fact that the dramatic emplotment of the game involves people coming together – *Lord of the Rings* (2007), for instance, requires players to join 'fellowships' and this makes sense, given what everyone knows about the story on which the game is based. Yee (2009) highlights the 'frequent occurrence of crises' in games, such as enemy or monster attacks, which he says promotes solidarity among players. These incentives to be sociable are reflected in key affordances of the games, especially the communication channels discussed previously, which players use to connect with one another in and out of the game. The nature of the communications in MMPGs varies but they all have designated channels through which players can either speak or send text to one or more other players. There are also discussion boards and other 'social forums', usually supported by the game publishers, to which players' subscription fees give them access. Here, players can communicate, normally asynchronously, outside of the game.

The nature of the in-game channels is articulated to the requirements of the game. In other words, the ludic structure of the game reaches through and shapes the communicative capacities of players in certain preferred directions. This is not to say that the design of the communication channels determines what players do – it does not. But it does limit the range of communicative actions that can be performed and, fused as it is with the rules of the game, it promotes certain kinds of communicative action. As Celia Pearce points out, game architectures contain 'embedded values' (Pearce 2009: 34, 73) that include the idea of social interaction and co-operation. This can be read as a case of what Peter-Paul Verbeek (2005) calls the 'moral agency of technology': the design of the game promotes a sociable disposition that corresponds to the intentions of its designers, who want people to play together.

The technical infrastructure fosters this activity in a number of ways. Pearce points to the fact that we can see our avatars on the screen in MMPGs, in contrast to other games that present a 'first person' perspective. This, she says, enhances the player's ability to project imaginatively, and their feeling of 'presence' in the world is thereby strengthened (Pearce 2009: 123). In her judgement, this is also a factor that contributes to the development of emotional ties between players, because in MMPGs we can see ourselves as others see us. Pearce describes how a community of players were formed in a prototype MMPG, URU, which closed down before it became publicly available. In her account, these players formed a gaming diaspora who migrated to other MMPGs, acquiring new members and remaining in contact. The events she describes, however, suggest that the diasporic identity itself became a kind of founding myth that contributed to the group's cohesion. The fact that URU never went live also seems to have been a factor, since in a sense the players had nothing but disappointed expectations, which allowed them to build a myth around *URU* – something that may not have been possible had they actually played there for an extended period and found that it was just another game. These possibilities are not considered by Pearce in her interpretation.

Other aspects of game architecture also promote social connection and facilitate recognition. It is difficult to advance one's avatar without joining up with others to embark on missions like hunting large monsters. More than this, however, connecting with others and institutionalizing the relationship (as a guild, fellowship, raiding party, or in gangster games a 'family') affords access to more specialized communication channels. These are used to communicate only with others in your group. This structure is particularly strong in *EverQuest*, where players must join guilds if they are to progress in the game and are obliged to keep their avatars' XP (experience points) within a specified range of that achieved by other guild members or face expulsion.

The articulation of sociable interaction to ludic objectives is weakened somewhat in *World of Warcraft*, in the sense that it offers less direct support for and encouragement of guilds and other collaborative activity. *WoW* players choose when creating their avatar to be in one of two clans: the alliance or the horde. Thereafter, they can communicate with others on the same side as them in the great conflict that marks that game world, while those on the other side see and hear only a scrambled version of their speech. However, *WoW* allows more scope for playing alone – Golumbia claims that most *WoW* gaming is 'for the individual' and many parts are 'played on one's own' (Golumbia 2009: 187) – than *EQ*, but the observation that collaboration is helpful to success in the game and so favoured in its design remains valid, especially in the later stages of the game when players have attained maximum XP, because 'completing' the game requires taking down an enemy that can only be defeated by a group of 40 or more players.

It is common for small guilds to be based on off-line friendships or kinship relations (75 per cent have some element of this; Williams et al. 2006). People use the games to stay in touch, perhaps parents and teenage children who have gone away to college, rather than to form new relationships. Viewing this as a straightforwardly benign extension of the domestic sphere is sociologically naïve. Studies show how the introduction of media technology into these relationships affects the balance of power within families, as discussed in the last chapter. Indeed, T.L. Taylor identifies part of the appeal of MMPGs in their power to liberate us from oppressive aspects of established friendship and family pools. There are reasons to be sceptical, therefore, of Williams et al.'s (2006) claim that small guilds not only connect people off-line but also correlate to specific ideological convictions, when they write that 'egalitarian organization and a dislike of military-style hierarchy, often reinforced through humor and sarcasm, were mainstays of the successful small guilds' (Williams et al. 2006: 347). Their own account actually suggests that there may be more going on in this word 'play' than the obvious value affirmations. Their principal observation, however, is that with growing size of guild comes reduced sociability and more formalization, including web-sites with mission statements, and other responsibilities. Leadership becomes important to maintaining these larger guilds and this can be experienced as quite burdensome.

The difficulty is that sociability that is leveraged into existence in this way actually lacks authenticity, and this limits its potential to tell us anything valid about ourselves. In terms of recognition, when we find that others acknowledge our acts as kind, effective or worthwhile, we know that in some measure our action and their perception of it were steered by the technological and ludic context in which we were operating. This amounts to a kind of erosion of the value of the recognition and consequently undermines its meaning when we afford it to others in response to their performances as well. The situation is akin to the kind of engineered 'positive' thinking associated with the culture industry, discussed in chapter 1. As we have seen, 'streamlined people' are encouraged to smile and think optimistic thoughts, regardless of how they really feel, or the facts of their situation, in the belief that this will be sufficient to turn events in their favour. Unfortunately, as Barbara Ehrenreich points out, with wages for working- and middle-class jobs falling and conditions of employment deteriorating for most people,

> the universe [has] refused to play its assigned role as a 'big mail order department.' In complete defiance of the 'law of attraction,' long propounded by the gurus of positive thinking, things . . . [are] getting worse for most Americans, not better. (Ehrenreich 2009: 178)

MMPGs also manipulate people into assuming a positive disposition, but here their prayers tend to be answered. If players are effective collaborators, they will experience the rewards of a certain kind of recognition and in-game success and status. The significance of this will always be difficult to fathom, however, and it is in this context that we should understand Yee's finding that more than half of the respondents in his study of *WoW* felt their leadership skills had improved as a result of playing the game. In a society that offers few real opportunities for people to show initiative and secure positive appreciation from others for this, MMPGs at least offer the appearance of something similar. This must be considered among the primary recuperative benefits to players of MMPGs.

It also provides the sociological context for the ambivalent character of the social connections formed in the game worlds. People are wedded to the notion that life is meritocratic and that if they work hard and put a brave face on things they will get their deserts. That the contemporary social and economic system does not, as a matter of objective fact, reward good behaviour in this way promotes disillusionment and disengagement. That MMPGs do reward active, positive participation makes them attractive, but only in the awareness that they are merely games. The activity and its rewards are located under a horizon of artificial constraints that compromises not only their economic value but their moral or ethical importance too.

The distorted recognition structures in MMPGs may explain why Williams et al. (2006) find that the kinds of attachments formed there had 'significant depth and bonding for a small portion of players' but that 'it was more common for players to consider their guild mates as something of a hybrid of tight real-life bonds and a group of relative strangers' (Williams et al. 2006: 352). Their observation is consistent with Sherry Turkle's (2010) suggestion that contemporary communications technologies leave us not really knowing what kind of tie we have with others – we seem to be always connected and so never alone, yet our multiple connections are thin and more people describe themselves as feeling lonely more of the time. As Turkle puts it, 'On networks, including game worlds, we are together but so lessen our expectations of other people that we can feel utterly alone' (2010: 226). The context for this is a networked society in which 'relentless connection leads to a new solitude'.

Bennerstedt and Ivarsson argue that MMPGs 'structure players' activities in that they have to adjust to certain ways of using the game in order to progress and to become a "normal" and accepted online citizen' (Bennerstedt and Ivarsson 2010: 203). However, it is doubtful that citizenship is the appropriate category for describing membership of MMPG society. These recognition conditions are compensatory and symptomatic rather than offering any kind of secure social foundation for critical thought or solidaristic political activity.

3. Ludefaction and the Diminution of Gameplay

The ludic underpinnings of social interaction in MMPGs mean that certain kinds of activity are rewarded and cash out in the positive esteem of other players. This is a drawn-out process with many phases. The activity of 'grinding', which involves repetitious actions at particular points in the game environment, enables players to accumulate in-game currency and items that can be used to enhance their status. 'Levelling up' in this way makes avatars more powerful. Clerics acquire access to a wider range of spells, for example, while warriors can wield more powerful weapons. Finally, these accruals of status facilitate the performance of more and greater feats in specific action sequences, which in turn secure the admiration and respect of other players. In the majority of games such achievements involve 'virtuoso' manoeuvres and sustained performances of skill in battle scenarios – Bennerstedt and Ivarsson refer to a choreography of avatar movement (2010: 223). Success in MMPGs is a matter of realizing the maximum capacities of the kind of avatar or type of character a player has chosen. A level 70 wood elf, for example, cannot aspire to perform the same feats with a mêlée weapon that a warrior class avatar could, while neither could run around at the periphery of a battleground adroitly casting spells to preserve their comrades. The struggle for recognition here is for acknowledgement of fulfilling the destiny appropriate to the type of creature one is; it concerns the realization of potentials that are tied to a specific social role in a social structure that is essentially static. As indicated above, this pattern of recognition is in marked contrast with the kind that Honneth associates with modern civil society. The kinds of action that are esteemed in MMPGs correspond more closely to the pre-modern concept of virtuous action, based on honour.

Perhaps unsurprisingly, then, there are no political mechanisms in MMPGs through which players might have a say in setting the rules of the game world. This lack of accountable governance structures contrasts with the kind of arrangements that used to exist in multi-user dungeons, or MUDs, the 1990s forerunners of MMPG worlds. Accounts of the

1992 LambdaMOO rape incident, for example, describe how players discussed the events and effectively mandated specific responses, including the ultimate eviction of the 'rapist' character, from the game 'wizards' – players with a direct connection to the technicians who manage the database. The move from not-for-profit on-line forum with (albeit flawed) democratic mechanisms to multi-million dollar playgrounds with exclusively corporate modes of governance mirrors developments in the wider world over the past three decades, especially those associated with the dominance of neo-liberal social and economic policies (Crouch 2011). As Sal Humphreys (2009) points out, the sole measure of good governance in MMPGs is continued profitability.

Humphreys argues that what is normally cast as 'player choice' to be creative, participate and so on can actually be interpreted as an effect of what she calls neo-liberal governance strategies. The 'ideal gamer identity' is one that participates as it consumes and this is fostered by 'rules and constraints which set very specific forms of challenges and goals' (Humphreys 2008: 154). I am making the related point that this kind of manipulation is made possible by recognition-deficits that ensure the forms of sociality specific to MMPGs are inherently limited and limiting. Humphreys argues that, in MMPGs, 'we witness new tactics and strategies for dealing with the messiness of new formations' (Humphreys 2008: 159), strategies that are in many ways illustrative of 'the shift towards private policing in many different areas and in ways that compromise privacy. Private police', she points out, 'are not subject to the same rigours of accountability as public police' (Humphreys 2008: 164). In MMPGs, the avatarial part of player identity is owned by the game publisher (Humphreys 2009; Ruch 2009). MMPGs are owned by corporations on the legal basis that they are services provided to players (Lastowka 2009).

The endemic confusion that pervades MMPGs leads some players to mistake themselves as representatives of the game. These players are recruited by the game company to 'police in-game behaviour' (Humphreys 2008: 160). They serve as guides and conflict-mediators in return for several hours of free play each week. In this way, the administrative work of providing player support, which could involve paying 20–40 employees, is now outsourced to unpaid workers. These kinds of strategies are common in MMPGs, another being the routine scrutiny of player discussion boards for free ideas about game improvements. As Humphreys says, this kind of practice 'represents a significant shift in the location of expertise between professionals and amateurs' (Humphreys 2008: 160). It is representative of a general tendency of neo-liberal management, which has often involved the displacement of paid professionals by non-credentialized, yet often highly skilled, cheap alternative labour.

Some critical theorists have suggested that the laws controlling the ownership of MMPGs should be changed, to reflect the fact that an MMPG is not simply 'code' that can be subject to proprietary controls applicable to other intellectual property, but a kind of 'space' (Ruch 2009). Humphreys calls for state regulation of life in MMPGs, to bring this part of society under the control of publicly accountable authorities, rather than being subject only to the narrow set of laws that concern intellectual property. Such reform has a rationale, but Humphreys' call runs up against the fact that it has no audience, no 'conditions of application' (Habermas 1995) in the sense that her analysis does not enable us to identify a constituency who might act on and give force to her demands. Reform of this kind would require a struggle for recognition waged through solidaristic association with others in the same predicament. It would involve making an appeal to the society beyond gamers to secure recognition of their structural position within the game. As Luc Boltanski (2011) has pointed out, one of the key functions of domination is to impose a structural differentiation of reality that ensures such struggles appear unrealistic. In this case, the mass of society will surely see the struggle of MMPGers as irrelevant. After all, they could simply choose not to play there. Moreover, the fact that their activity is defined as play, that the identities they assume there are ludic and that inter-player recognition is itself based on the kinds of designed limitation and distortion discussed above, means that the idea of them lobbying for change is difficult to take seriously – indeed, Humphreys does not suggest that it will happen. Nonetheless, the question raised by these critics, and posed most clearly by Adam Ruch, is surely apposite: 'What does this weird concept of space-as-service, or service-as-space, do to the concept of self, autonomy and personal or public liberty?' (Ruch 2009).

In the recognition-theoretic analysis advanced here, the answer is that MMPGs are part of a cultural context that blunts the force of those concepts in a fairly systematic way. The new spirit of capitalism creates conditions under which the kinds of recognition necessary for us to feel and act like citizens with rights are prevented because we never obtain a clear-sighted perspective on ourselves and others.

It was the print revolution in Europe that led to the emergence of the first public sphere. Moveable type made it easy to produce reliable copies of documents that could circulate widely, carrying the same message to disparate locations. As the first medium of mass communication, print was also an important agent of enlightenment, distributing scientific findings and, more importantly, laying the foundations for the production of new knowledge. The new forms of sociality that characterized early modern Europe were intimately connected to the rise of a scientific consciousness and a new role for the rigorous pursuit of truth in human affairs.[15] This alliance of political consciousness and knowledge was ambiguous in the sense that it was also the crucible of a new alliance of knowledge and strategies of domination. Foucault's (1985) analysis of the panopticon is often viewed as a key text in helping us understand this new historical formation. It reveals the imbrication of a methodology for producing truth, through systematic, measured and repeated observation that is, each step of the way, also a mechanism of containment and coercion. The prisoner in his cell is observed and studied by a mechanism which forces him into a certain way of being: the criminal's truth is an effect of the panoptic regime.

Early studies of cyberspace highlighted the possibility that on-line spaces might be used to create an 'electronic panopticon' (Gordon 1987; Mathieson 1997), in which digital technologies would be used to intensify surveillance and enhance social domination. In MMPGs, however, we discover an important modification of panopticism, in which the logic that ties truth to power is modified by others, namely, those of the game and of the fetishized commodity. The combination of these factors gives rise to a new model, which I call the phenakisticon. Like the panopticon, the phenakisticon combines viewing technologies with strategies of domination. Unlike them, it does not attempt to force new truths out of darkness but rather foments confusion (*phenakisein* – to deceive; *icon* – image, portrayal) in a strategy that is manipulative and involves moments of pleasure. Life in the phenakisticon presupposes and encourages cynicism on the part of the people it casts as players. They are knowingly deceived but, unable to act on a truth that might dispel the illusion, play on regardless.

We have seen that MMPGs create an environment in which recognition is uncertain and self-respect is based in practices whose very respectability is dubious, and perhaps enjoyed as such – there is a wry humour in being esteemed as a high-ranking wood elf. The cynicism thus solicited might be corrosive to the game's project. Millions of pounds are spent to ensure that wood elves look fantastic and are, in a sense, 'believable'. The game positions its players in this ambiguous territory, inviting them to hack away at a carefully prepared illusion. Moreover, playing the game involves acquiring facets of self that one does not fully believe in and developing relationships that carry an intense charge even though they are, in all likelihood, transient and likely to be superficial in the fuller context of one's personal biography. A recognition-theoretic approach enables us to see that MMPGs encourage sociality but only under conditions that limit its significance and disorientate its participants. Participation requires a certain self-abnegation, a loss of credibility in one's own eyes, but this is not bought through straightforward deception. There is an inherent pleasure in being steered into sociability, helping and being helped, even when we know that these things are not quite what they seem to be. These pleasures are real but they are not what we initially take them to be. The effect of the phenakisticon is to confer a kind of levity and imaginative charge on contemporary social relations that makes them more bearable, even as it makes the prospects for solidaristic and imaginative action to change society more remote than ever.

For some, however, it is actually a mistake to interpret the activity in MMPGs as play at all. From this perspective, the instrumentalization of human affairs that critical theory detected in the first culture industry is the dominant feature of MMPG organization, and this is one of the most disturbing features of in-game activity. David Golumbia (2009), for instance, argues that far from being cultures based on play, life in MMPGs is very like 'work' in the digital economy. As T.L. Taylor puts it, 'our playtime is increasingly intersecting with work and productive activities' (Taylor 2006: 89). Other economic analyses (Castronova 2005; Heeks 2010) have shown that activity in MMPGs has 'real-world' economic functions. There are multiple aspects to this claim, some of which reprise issues discussed in the previous chapter. Player activity creates the game, produces a product that players then pay for, generating profits for the corporation that owns the process. Players' experiments and role playing extend the life of the products and may even be a source of ideas for game designers' future projects. Gamers' data profiles are used for marketing of future games and other, related products.

Beyond this, in-game artefacts are traded on real-world markets. Gold farmers grind away the hours to gather currency which is then sold on international markets for real currency. Gold farming is an organized business overwhelmingly located in China, to such an extent that the Chinese New Year is almost guaranteed to produce a shortage of game currency and a spike in prices. As Richard Heeks (2010) shows, the returns on the practice are always diminishing, so that game currencies resemble those of failing real-world ones.[16] There have even been reports of prisoners in China being forced to work as gold farmers for their gaolers (Vincent 2011).

Castronova (2005) opposes these kinds of development to what he sees as a game culture that is worth defending in the face of its colonization by 'real-world' economic processes. However, this culture is itself one in which the play is primarily turned inwards and directed at the generative structures of culture itself. What we find in MMPGs is not productive play of the social imaginary, but more a play with that imaginary and with the possibility that it might ever be truly productive – of new kinds of self-respect, of real mutual recognition, or of solidarity. Here, it is significant that in newer MMPGs, gameplay ceases to function as the standard evaluative criterion. WoW is illustrative here. Success in this game is achieved by spending as much time here as everyone else and by performing broadly the same number of dull procedures as them. Linderoth and Bennerstedt (2007) quote one player as saying that the game is 'unbelievably boring' (2007: 44) without social interaction with other players. The game does not present players with real challenges but rather rewards the investment of time: 'time invested gives a reward in terms of status. A player with no playing ability can still gain status' (2007: 51). In this, WoW resembles social media, especially Facebook, which reward social 'success', measured in terms of numbers of 'friends', with more social success, reflected in the same shallow measurement operation (cf. Keen 2012).[17]

Participation in game procedures and the maintenance of social connections here supersede gameplay and displace gaming discourse. For some, this constitutes the 'ludification' of social relationships. But this phraseology is misleading because what is actually happening is the annulment of games, in their joyful ebullience, and of gameness as a quasi-autonomous cultural practice. Drawing on an adaptation of geological metaphors, I would like to contrast ludification with ludefaction, in the way that geologists speak not of liquification but of the more hazardous liquefaction. Liquefaction involves dry substances turning fluid as the result of a collapse of internal micro-structures. It is associated with the reverberations caused by earthquakes or hazardous mining activities. Liquefaction can cause subsidence and damage to surface structures. Ludefaction may pose a similar threat via the psychic and cultural substructures that are necessary for human creativity and cultural life. Golumbia sums up the ramifications of this extremely well:

> Rather than an imaginary economy 'bleeding over' into reality, . . . it seems more productive to understand phenomena like *WoW* and *EQ* as extensions of physical economies into our own ideological imaginaries, much like movies and television before them. Unlike most movies and television, however, MM[OR]PGs demand intimate and profound engagement from individual users. The popular name for this phenomenon is addiction. (Golumbia 2009: 196)

The 'thick schizophrenia' (Hayot and Wesp 2009) of MMPGs consists in a dispersal of the energies of play across the field of relationships in MMPGs. This pleasurable charge is at the same time a deceitful sheen; the dynamics of the process are those of a commodification of recognition and mutual respect. As I have tried to argue here, the implications for solidarity are largely negative, since in the phenakisticon we can be sure neither of ourselves nor of each other but are seduced into collaborating only to the extent that this serves the dominant social interest, namely, the one that the corporation has in keeping the game going.

CHAPTER SIX

Aesthetics and Politics

I have presented computer games as part of a broad set of changes affecting the character of capitalist economies, society and technology over the last 40 years. Following Boltanski and Chiapello (2005), the original impetus for these changes has been traced to the 'artistic critique' of capitalism in the 1960s. This critique succeeded in transforming the feel of life in capitalist societies. It created a situation in which the brutality and boredom of industrial capitalism were replaced by forms of labour that efface the work/leisure distinction. However, the critique failed in that the exploitative logic of the capitalist social system has not been reformed but intensified. As we have seen in the last two chapters, even our unremunerated play is now liable to be harnessed and turned into a source of economic value by game (and other) corporations. This kind of manipulation has implications too for the social imaginary, as the notion of a space that is not subordinate to the demands of capital becomes difficult to sustain. Increasingly, our play is a kind of toying with the possibility of authentic and meaningful connection. System imperatives reach through all our activities and threaten to encroach upon areas of personal life and social relationships, undermining the psycho-social bases of respect and solidarity.

At the same time, however, gaming has been shown to have recuperative functions. The very fact that people continue to seek and find pleasure through play is what makes many of the new forms of exploitation possible. Gaming is a quasi-autonomous cultural practice in the sense that it has forced normative and evaluative categories into public discourse that are not reducible to the needs and interests of corporations but can occasionally be used to challenge them. Gamers can express frustration at the endless tide of sequels; they can flout restrictions on their ludic activities, and they can defy proprietorial boundaries on game objects. In so doing they can enjoy the recognition and respect of other gamers, which are based on the skills of gameplay and assignments of intrinsic value to the activity. Gaming culture, then, is both a site of domination in contemporary capitalism and one of recuperation, perhaps even critique, albeit in this very restricted sense.

'Gameplay' condenses a novel kind of experience, a new combination of sensations and performances, and, once established, the concept facilitates the inscription and dissemination of this experience in social practice. To understand what it is, though, we need to explore its subjective aspect by looking at what playing games feels like. It may seem odd to connect this question of the subjective, experiential side of gaming with politics and the question of the political significance of the spread of gaming as a cultural practice. However, it is through investigation of what computer games feel like to play (their aesthetics) that we unearth their political dimension.

The most important thing about computer games is not their content, if this is understood to mean a message that is transmitted and then interpreted by audiences. A study of self-identified gamers by the British Board of Film Classification (BBFC 2005), for instance, shows that for most players the storyline element of games is not particularly important,[1] despite the emphasis in games marketing on the cinematic characteristics of contemporary games. Movie audiences do not report lack of interest in plot, story and character. Computer games differ from traditional media primarily because of the central role of play in their consumption. Media researchers cannot offer valid interpretations of games by watching recordings of other people playing them; it is necessary to play them to experience their distinctive effects and characteristic limitations. The very assumption that *Manhunt* (2003) is a 'violent' game, for example, overlooks the specific mediations that make *Manhunt* a game, before it is a book, or a film, or anything that imparts a narrative 'about' something else. Similarly, we would be foolish to assume that *The Naughty One* (1984) was 'about' sex, simply because of the title and packaging that came with the product.[2] There are mediations that are specific to computer games and which mostly concern player practices and activities that have no parallel in connection with other popular culture media and other kinds of audience.[3]

If we want to understand what games signify to players, we need to attend first to what players do with them and to the distinctive processes they engage in with them. The fact that we *play* with games powerfully conditions our interpretation of their meaning and perhaps limits the significance we can attach to them (see Kirkpatrick 2011). It also positions the activity in a distinctive relationship with the social imaginary because, as we saw in the previous chapter, the nature of social connection is altered when it goes on against a ludic background. At the same time, computer gaming is, or can be, a meaningful practice for those engaged in it. Their engagement touches upon and shapes their identity. As we saw in chapter 3, being a gamer involves seeking recognition from others, and contemporary gaming offers forms of participation in different kinds of imagined community. There is an important relationship here between the aesthetics of gameplay and political questions of personal identity and social solidarity.

This chapter begins by trying to define the computer game aesthetic, focusing particularly on embodied play. Playing a game is an active performance that is only possible for someone who has habituated themselves to gameplay as a subjective possibility. For this, they must have stretched their sensory configurations in specific directions and twisted their bodily dispositions so that a joystick, for example, has become a familiar object, and no explanation is needed regarding the role of the fingers in affecting what happens on screen. It is in the way that games work on us and the embodied responses we discover and learn that computer game aesthetics must be located. The pragmatic approach to defining games adopted in the current work enables us to pin down a particular combination of media elements in connection with a system of perceptions and practices (gamer *habitus*) as definitive, or constitutive, for the medium. This definition attaches particular importance to the embodied activity of the player and its occasionally dissonant relation to what is projected on the game screen.

The second section positions the aesthetic character of games thus understood in terms of changes to the social imaginary associated with the broad historical changes that, as the rest of this book has discussed, define the context for the development of computer games and gaming. This requires reflection on the contemporary meaning of aesthetic experience and art, and of the changing relation of these to the idea of critique. Playing a game involves a kind of distantiation from its narrative components, or conventional interpretations of its symbolic contents. This distance is often open to ironic inflection, although it is rarely (if ever) critical. It corresponds to the changed structural position of the aesthetic in a society where, as I indicated at the end of the last chapter, the radical imaginary faces new pressures. Critique lacks a stable background against which it can draw out the vision of an alternative society based on different values. Under these circumstances, we also see a changed role for the aesthetic and for art, which can no longer rely on drawing critical contrasts to make its point.

The distinctive gaming aesthetic described in the first section becomes the basis, in the final section, for reflection on how games and gaming might serve a critical function. The discussion is informed by Jacques Rancière's (2009a) idea of the 'emancipated spectator' and his concept of 'subjectivation'. It is in the way that games separate us from common-sense interpretations of experience that we find a close parallel with the critical potentials of art. Like visitors to art galleries, gamers are subjects of a process that involves a distinctive relation to the social imaginary. In both cases, there is a sense that the 'as if' character of their experiences converges with the sense of contingency in social arrangements that is necessary if they are to take steps towards emancipation. Unlike them, however, for gamers the resulting sensibility is not one that involves a sense of the universality of this capacity, or of its equal accessibility to anyone whatsoever. This discussion identifies what I see as the central ambivalence of computer games as a cultural form and it concludes the book.

1. The Aesthetic Dimension

Computer games are not representational systems in the straightforward sense that their meaning content can be read off from their visual narrative or textual elements. The very assertion, 'it's only a game', often heard in debates about violence, for instance, invokes the deeper understanding that we do not actually know what our gameplay is 'about' and that most of the time it does not really matter: being about something, or representation, is not the principal way that meaning works in play with games. The temptation to develop games with strongly provocative themes, like the confusion over whether gameplay is just childish or 'can be' something more respectable and grown up, are underscored by this ambiguity.

As Susana Tosca (2003) has pointed out, games resemble the high arts in their form, but in their embodied dimension and their emphasis on movement, they are connected to low, or popular, culture. This observation aligns games with dance. Both involve the body in potentially transgressive ways, and in both cultural forms the relation to meaning, to communicative content, is distanced and subject to distinctive rules. Dance does not have to 'mean' anything in order to communicate. We appreciate the tensions, strength and grace in the dancer's body through an obscure process of empathic intuition. Even though there are some rules concerning dance as a communicative practice, like the principle that gestures of the arms are more expressive than those of the lower half of the body, the meaning of a dance is intuited rather than interpreted. The obscurity is perhaps similar to that of games, in that in each case the element of embodied performance is key to the pleasures of the activity.

Dance Dance Revolution (DDR), for example, is an arcade game made by Konami in 1998. It involves players matching their feet to illuminated squares on a metal platform, in time to music. The game is competitive, in that you receive a points score for avoiding error and hitting the right squares at the right time. However, in his study of the phenomenon, Bryan Behrenshausen (2007) finds that players also enjoy the activity merely for the element of embodied movement. For them, he writes, this performance is 'part of a game text with no overarching narrative and no ultimate end-state – a game whose object is simply to perform, and perform well' (Behrenshausen 2007: 339). I have argued that the dissociative character of all video gameplay fits this description, although hand-held controllers stage the activity in a smaller area (Kirkpatrick 2009). The logic of embodied performance is the same – a point Behrenshausen also makes.

Acknowledging the dance character of gameplay subverts the hold of 'game' as a definition of the activity. According to Behrenshausen, players say that they see the game as *both* dancing and a game. The activity is also inherently social, or intersubjective. Behrenshausen's respondents discuss how they compare performances and are aware of one another's scores as well as of their own sensations and of the game machine as a kind of competitor:

> When playing *DDR*, these players are conscious of their relationships with bodies other than that of the machine; indeed, this consciousness helps them retain something essential to the perpetual enjoyment of play. (2007: 346)

This pleasurable dimension is part of what makes gameplay attractive, even though it may not normally be thematized as such by players: they do not persuade each other to participate with words, but through performance itself.

As we have seen, the discovery of gameplay coincides with a tightening of the link between the body of the gamer and the controller as a part of the gaming apparatus. The sociological autonomy of gaming and its self-understanding as a legitimate and valid thing to do were secured when the gamer *habitus* was formed around the controller. Eugénie Shinkle (2008) has also argued that understanding the pleasures of gameplay requires attentiveness to the body and, in particular, to the proprioceptive sense. This is the sense we have of the ways in which we are disposed within our own bodies. The feelings we derive from gameplay are, she writes, 'a function not just of on-screen events, but of the physical activity of gameplay itself' (Shinkle 2008: 907). Shinkle suggests that there is a change in terms of the range of expression afforded by newer full-body motion interfaces, especially the *Wii*, but this obscures their real significance. Like hand-held controllers, they demand movement (and not 'more' of that!) tailored to situations. These innovations to controller design do modify the gamer *habitus* and, as I have argued (Kirkpatrick 2009), this has been important in drawing in new audiences, especially women, to the pleasures of console gaming. What we see here are, as Shinkle says, different kinds of incorporation, but as Patrick Crogan (2010) points out, the *Wii*-mote by no means abandons the priority afforded to manual dexterity and virtuosity in the traditional gamer *habitus*. The significance of the new controllers does not lie in expanding the expressive or emotional content of the gameplay experience,[4] but in the different repertoire of physical actions required to play and the sensations associated with this. The body is central to computer game aesthetics, and understanding what games are requires that we focus on the intersection of this embodied activity on one side and the other elements of the game on the other.

Drawing on Richard Shusterman's (2008) idea of a 'somaesthetics', Henrik Smed Nielsen argues that video games resemble art in the way that they 'both require a certain self-abnegating sensibility in order to become part of its relations' (Nielsen 2010: 30). Both art and games involve 'a perceptual and somatic sensibility' that we work on in the course of our engagement and which alters us in the process. The repetitions of gameplay thus have to be seen as part of a cyclical reverberation between elements of gameplay that involve what Nielsen calls 'decoupling', as against those that are 'naturalized'. Running through the experience of playing a game is a tension, or 'clash' (2010: 33), between two bodies: the corporeal body of the player and the avatarial form that represents the player 'in' the game, normally on its screen. At various stages in any given game, the 'naturalized' responses of the player – the ones that have been habituated perhaps from the start of the game – get 'decoupled' from their previous associations and connections. This happens, for example, in *Resident Evil 5* (2009), when the image of a controller button appears on screen to tell you that this button now has a specific function (usually to dodge an attack) that it does not normally have. These incidents create scope for new kinds of performance and re-naturalization of actions; in each case there is a new mapping of embodied performance to the requirements of the script. These kinds of jump, each of them a small modification of procedure within player *habitus*, are central to the enjoyment of gameplay essentially because decoupling and the struggle to regain habituated control are amusing (Nielsen 2010: 35). They can be enjoyed as a challenge, appreciated by others as comic, especially in cases of ridiculous failure, and savoured as performance. As Nielsen points out, in the latter case there is consciousness on the part of performer and audience alike[5] of the discipline and restraint that have subordinated straightforward 'expression' to produce something much more like a dance. He argues that 'simultaneous decoupling and naturalisation "changes" or "restructures" me and my playing', and this also aligns gameplay with art, a point to which I will return below.

Grasping the aesthetic specificity of computer games in this way is essential if we are to fix the identity of the computer game at this point in history and in this culture. As we have seen, the computer game includes a game apparatus (controller, computer running a program, screen, etc.) that had to be incorporated into a field of cultural practice where it has been consolidated in the habits and perceptions of people who, in part, identify themselves with it. The subjective side of this process includes the performances and experiences codified in gaming discourse as *gameplay*, as well as endless effort to clarify the merits of that elusive quality. As Shinkle points out, full clarification of 'gameplay' is probably impossible in principle:[6]

> [G]ameplay is difficult to describe, and this resistance to theorization is seen by many as an obstacle to be overcome. Within both industry and academia, gameplay (and perception, more broadly) continues, for the most part, to be discussed in terms of vision, visuality, and rational decision-making. In fact, gameplay comprises a much more complex mesh of perceptual activity, and the limitations of the present vocabulary are a testimony to those elements of gameplay that language cannot properly address. (Shinkle 2008: 909)

The repeated crashes and defeats of gaming and the circuitous and extraneous nature of gameplay when viewed in terms of ostensible game narratives seem to promote a kind of pleasurable disorientation,[7] one that is profoundly consonant with Boltanski and Chiapello's observation that there is a widespread 'confusion about the meaning of everyday existence' (2005: 424). The narrative in a game may involve overcoming a succession of opponents and obstacles in order to experience a movie-like 'cut-scene' in which we are rewarded in some way for our efforts. But to achieve that outcome, we do not think like a racing car driver, or a magical elf, or a warehouse man – their problems are not the ones we engage with as we puzzle out what to do next and work on doing it fast enough. There is a recurrent disconnect between the narrative theme and the kinds of activity we engage in with the aim (which can be more or less foregrounded in our thinking) of driving the narrative on. Commonly, we have to spend some time thinking about the controller and what we have to do with our hands to be successful and, in such phases of gameplay, there is no question of being immersed in a fictional role, or often even of allowing one's eyes to look into the game as a visually presented world or spectacle. In difficult games, this switching of attention between elements of the apparatus is so frequent and necessary to success that players completely forget the significance of their actions in terms of the fictional narrative, focusing instead on achieving success with the task (literally and figuratively) at hand.

The PS3 game, *Journey* (2012), offers an exceptionally smooth experience of gameplay, but it is still fundamentally dissonant in the sense presented here. You take control of a veiled figure in a red cape who moves gracefully through a desert-like environment. Progress depends upon learning to fly, which involves issuing whale-like calls to clouds of small red rectangles, which respond by swirling around you and lifting you into the air. Larger rectangles resemble carpets and at times in the game you can ride these through the air, above the mysterious structures below. At other times there are machines like big tape dispensers that have to be called into life, by touching them, at which point carpet-like bridges appear and allow you to cross the various chasms you encounter. Your journey is to the highest mountain-top, which is present in the distance throughout the game. Failure in this game consists in sliding into a kind of underworld where there are flying, robot-like machines spitting electric discharge, which crash into you and diminish your flying capabilities. These moments in the game are disorientating but, intriguingly, you do not die, as would be the case in a conventional game.

It might seem as if this game was inconsistent with the model of dissonance I have been presenting, but even here we find the distantiations and discrepancies that give gameplay its characteristic tension. For one thing, the game's symbolism is deeply abstract. Your avatar is recognizably human but has no distinguishing characteristics, so that when you meet another player it is possible to become confused as to which character is yours. The environment, with its ruins, flags and carpets, is also recognizably that: a playspace with structures that do not represent anything else. The idea of a journey is set against a background that is deliberately generic in all of its particulars. The fact that there is no speech or text in the game enhances the purity of the gameplay: the tension between narrative and ludic activity is placed in abeyance because the whole question of reference or narrative meaning has been set aside. The emphasis is entirely on the forms traced out by your efforts with the controller in conjunction with the images and sounds of the game, and these latter offer resistance that varies in kind and intensity: you might have to press 'circle' repeatedly and vigorously, or just steer very carefully with the stick. The gameplay is particularly sweet when you are trying to climb through a sequence of fluttering flags, to reach a high plateau or move higher up the mountain. Even after you have realized that there is no death in this game, the feeling of an impending failure underscoring the activity persists and drives you on.

Viewed aesthetically, it is important to focus on how dissonance works within computer games, since this is what determines how they feel to players. What we find in gameplay is always the superimposition of a concrete, sensed experience on top of an initial appearance that is consistent with the idea of the game as a representation upon which we can act. The play of computer games is located in the dissonance between these levels.[8]

2. Art, Play and Critique

This analysis positions gameplay at a strange point in cultural life: it is a site in which we indulge our facility for enjoying sensations and permutations of sensible experience for their own sake. Structurally, this is similar to the location of art. As Theodor Adorno (2002) pointed out, the artwork is a site of play in a society otherwise dominated by work and the imperative always to be doing something purposive, or things that 'make sense'. Engaging with art, we allow ourselves to be playful and to be played with as a condition of extracting anything from the experience, which means we temporarily allow ourselves to be more childlike in our openness to the new and potentially strange. At the same time, the meanings we derive from the experience of opening up to art are serious and perhaps inherently inaccessible to children.[9] Art speaks to us about things we try to keep at bay in our conscious, organized lives, like mortality, the utter contingency of most of what we take for granted and the possibility of a more fulfilling way of life. Fundamentally perhaps, art speaks to us about the desirability of allowing imagination to infuse social orderings and, as such, it is a kind of questioning of the social imaginary.

Games are also the locus of a kind of play and, as such, they involve activity that does not 'make sense' in terms of the normal standards of adult behaviour. As I indicated previously, this probably explains why gaming as a cultural practice persistently hovers at the margin of respectability. Even after half a century, computer games still raise questions for players about the meaning of their activity. The questions of what games are and of what the value of the activity of gameplay is persist in contemporary gaming culture. A recent 'soapbox' discussion on the *Gamespot* web-site, for example, probes this theme. Responding to the suggestion that music is only an incidental feature of games, the author, Kevin Vanard, writes:

> to dismiss an important aspect of the gaming experience as inessential undermines it; after all, games themselves are non-essential. We do not need them to function; they do not provide physical warmth . . . or nourishment . . . Yet, like fine art, and literature, and love, and all the creature comforts that make our lives extraordinary, games entertain and enrich us. (Vanard 2011)

This kind of existential reflection on gaming is not unusual in popular discussions in the gaming press. It would, of course, be completely out of place in connection with other 'culture industry' products, like soap operas. In gamer forums and in much of the academic writing on games, it is also common to encounter a kind of frustration not just with the fact that we don't know what games are (yet), but also with their seeming inability to be (or get recognized as) something better, something more obviously valuable – like art.

For critical theorists concerned with the first culture industry, art's significance lay in the fact that it still offered a foothold for critique. In essence, this foothold was the tradition of art itself. The residual presence of ideas about beauty and form in a culture dominated by powerful forces dedicated to subordinating these things to marketing and manipulation was sufficient basis for modern art practice to gain some traction. Modern art was critical in the dual sense that it opposed mainstream culture (Arnold Schoenberg's challenging and dissonant compositions, for example, were a direct challenge to popular musical tastes and his works were presented by the composer himself as a call from the future), while at the same time it is always turned against itself as 'art'. Its superiority to popular trash is not a function of its being more beautiful but is rather manifest in its vulnerability to, even its mutilation by, the prevailing historical trends.

This is the context for Adorno's assertion that modern art 'abjures semblance' (2002: 154). The modernist aesthetic strategies of shock, montage and abstraction all testify to an aesthetic impulse that can no longer be contained within available meanings. This too has a dual sense: literal communication under these conditions is impossible because any attempt to represent will merely be assimilated and corrupted by the culture industry; the excess of human feeling and imagination cannot be contained in images that 'make sense' in conventional terms. Modern art aims to stir up in us that sensibility evoked by Martin Heidegger in his (2002 [1950]) essay on technology, namely, that there is something terribly wrong with the world we have created for ourselves but part of the terror is that we are unable to formulate it. The anguish and torment of modernist works speak to this excess of the (repressed) human under the conditions imposed by the culture industry.

Adorno likened artworks to puzzles (2002: 121). When we encounter them, we enjoy being surprised, finding the unexpected. Further curiosity leads to more surprises. In this way, we open up our latent potential for new kinds of experience and novel performances through which we can grow and change. In modern artworks, the element of form was opposed to that of representation. Art 'went radical' by turning in on itself. This was effective because it pointed beyond the work to the world, which was thereby indicted with preventing art from finding any resolution within itself. In the culture industry, the attempt to communicate a meaning leads directly to its incorporation in the system of messages that manipulate and pacify. The modern artwork presents itself almost as an accusation directed at the world, which has negated its meaning-making capacities. This message cannot be assimilated and used as part of an advertising strategy.

In our activity with computer games, we encounter dissonance repeatedly, as an effect of the combination of media elements in them and the resulting conflict of sensory modalities in play. However, games cannot be interpreted as extensions of artistic modernism because the tension they maintain is internal – in terms of the form we experience in them, or the gameplay element, each game only speaks to us about itself. Even abstract games do not suggest any external deficiency that inhibits them from becoming beautiful representations. Rather, their failure to represent is built into them from the outset, so to speak, as a function of their gameness. Drawing on ideas from Gilles Deleuze, Christian Ulrik Andersen (2012) has pointed out that gameplay follows a 'logic of sensation'. Its coherence is not a matter of signification, in which the work represents something else, but of 'manifestation'. The performance of the player makes manifest a distinctive kind of meaning inherent in the relation between the player's body and the game text. The central premise of old-style critical theory was that critique represented a kind of excess in relation to the order imposed on the world by a rationalizing social system. The practical implication of this was that successful criticisms formulated through art might stimulate and even inform political action aimed at willed social transformation. Clearly, games cannot aspire to this kind of critique.

However, regardless of the limitations of gaming aesthetics, it seems that art itself seems to have lost its critical capacities in the new capitalism. As Lash and Lury point out, much contemporary art appears to have succumbed to the logic of commodification, resulting in what they call a 'meltdown of aesthetic value' (2007: 74). Contemporary art exhibits a knowing attitude towards the perpetuation of art as an institution under capitalism. It is cynical about art's capacity to communicate about anything other than itself and in some cases artworks are presented essentially as adverts for their creators, who have become 'brands' – TV personalities, pundits wheeled out to pontificate on issues of the day, from the elevated position of 'artist', which they themselves satirize. In essence, much art today has become a joke about art.

This reflects new cultural conditions associated with digital technology. There is a crisis affecting the social imaginary; the backdrop against which critique sets out its vision of an alternative way of life. Figuratively, it is as if the canvas available to traditional critical theorists has been replaced by an infinite number of unstable points which work together to produce a sense of the context of human action that is always too mobile and fluid to allow us to identify and establish patterns that might be more meaningful to people than the always already new, yet solid and unquestionable, social reality. As Boltanski (2011) puts it, critique is always running to catch up with reality: we face an excess of the real. Observing that contemporary radical sentiment is not at a low point, only its ability to gain any practical purchase (2011: 158), he writes:

> What critique as a collective enterprise currently lacks is doubtless not so much critical energy, present among a large number of people, as a *background* against which it could break loose and take *form* (to borrow an image from *Gestalt psychologie*), as if it has no sooner been formulated than it is integrated into the formats that give material substance to reality in its public dimensions. (Boltanski 2011: 41. Emphasis in original)

The problem is that the social imaginary no longer produces a space but proliferates a dynamic, shifting mass of points (something that is also implicit in Lash and Lury's characterization of it as a 'virtual' that has to be instantiated). To raise a 'critique' means advancing an alternative gestalt and submitting it to tests, inscribing it in a collective as an alternative reality. Games, by definition, cannot do this, because they are 'only' games. In all probability, however, neither can anything else, including art. The problem is this excess of the real.

This change in the objective context relates to the broad theme of this book, the entanglement of computer games in the transformation of capitalism over the last four decades. As we have seen, the artistic critique of the 1960s has succeeded in transforming technology and with it the labour process and working environments. Contemporary domination rests on an inherent mesh of neo-liberal ideology with most people's experience of work, mainly because it appeals to the streamlined individual's sense that they are responsible for their own lives. Work today is not only technologically determined grind but is also infused with the sheen of play and the promise of 'victory'. Critique cannot oppose humanity, nature or art to technology because technology has been transformed. The bugbear of traditional critical theory, 'technological rationality' is no longer in 'hegemonic' alignment with capitalist interests (Kirkpatrick 2008).

Critique is disorientated by this transition because it requires categorical distinctions upon which basis people can question the legitimacy of an arrangement or situation. Viewed as a critical form, computer games might be seen as allegories of the situation in which such distinctions are difficult to draw because the background conditions are too volatile; social reality is too viscous. In games, the player is the victim of an intrigue that is coded into the world itself, and thought cannot find anything beneath the evident contingency of this reality, upon which it might be able to offer an alternative thematization of experience. Instead we struggle to understand and overcome one set of challenges only to be presented with another. We do not believe the illusion; we know it is just an illusion, but we play along anyway because there is nothing else to do. Our overall progress with a game is paradoxical: we move towards using the game up (an empty victory) while the condition of this is further submission to its demands for more effort and concentration.

3. Critical Gaming?

For Jacques Rancière, this situation marks the end of critique,[10] but it does not terminate the radical oppositional function of art. For him, art is one of a number of practices that can promote dissensus by breaking us away from the consensually defined real and present alternative configurations of sensible experience. The distribution of sensible experience or the way we make sense from sense data is a political question because it concerns how we are unequally disposed in the world even prior to the process whereby political and ideological discourses take hold of our experiences and have their effects. In his analysis of art images, for example, the emphasis is not on the pictorial, visual character of the image as such, but its position in relation to how the visual sense is habitually used in our society and culture. The real significance of 'image' is a historically specific way of connecting words and visual representations. These 'distributions of the sensible' are 'regimes': they express and give form to relations of power and inequality.

The art image is defined by a particular kind of dissensus, through which artworks change how we use our visual sense to make sense:

> Images change our gaze and the landscape of the possible if they are not anticipated by their meaning and do not anticipate their effects. (Rancière 2009a: 105)

As Rancière puts it, art images separate sense from sense. Art involves curiosity and forces us to pay attention, as we enter 'dispositions of the body and the mind where the eye does not know in advance what it sees and thought does not know what it should make of it' (Rancière 2009a: 105). His clearest illustration of this is his argument that, contrary to a common, culturally conservative view that is salient on the political left, we are not living under a deluge of visual images such that discrimination, discernment (and ethics) are overwhelmed. Rather, it is the regime in which visuality is currently implicated that is problematic, because it assigns visual images to the masses, most strikingly the poor and the starving, who thereby become anonymous, while elite perspectives are expressed in words. The rich and powerful get to provide narratives – stories through which they express their individuality. This is how images work in our society: our social imaginary is pre-structured by the prevailing distributions of sense. Network society's orderings of visual representations and words or stories means that we live within 'embodied allegories of inequality' (2009: 12).

The distribution of sensible experience and the way we make sense from sensory experience is a political question because it concerns the ways we are unequally disposed in the world even prior to the processes whereby political and ideological discourses take hold of our experiences and have their effects. An example of this might be the Occupy movement, which subverted the dominant distribution of sensible experience in city centre spaces around the world. Creating human living spaces in places reserved for the 'serious' business of banking and political decision making makes us aware that the sorting of spaces, people and times is political before it is codified in discourse or law. There is nothing particularly 'realistic' about finance capitalism, but particular sensible orderings can make it seem paradigmatic. A very vivid demonstration of the politics of the sensible was provided in Britain in late 2011, when police helicopters used infra-red cameras to film the Occupy site in London and suggested that very few people were actually sleeping there overnight. This challenged the reality (and the realism) of the protest, reasserting the policed conception of the sensible and trying to confirm its authority as the only way things can really be.

Viewed in this way, the significance of the art image and the way its politics lie in it being at odds with regimes of the sensible that are particular or biased. What's important about art, according to Rancière, is that it can puncture our acceptance of this situation as the only possible configuration, or distribution, of sensible experience. This is not in the manner of the modernist *avant garde* or street theatre aimed at creating shocks, but rather through working on our sensorium to produce experiences that are intelligible yet not subject to conventional sense-making, or interpretation.

It is the equality of art's image that privileges art for emancipatory thought. The art image is one that is open to all on the same terms but experienced differently by each; the *sine qua non* of art is that everyone has their own interpretation and each knows that everyone else also has an interpretation. Rancière calls this the capacity of the art image to 'bring us together in being apart' – a striking inversion of Sherry Turkle's diagnosis of our present condition as one in which we are 'alone together', discussed in the previous chapter. Art's primary effect is to break up the hold of the dominant structuring of the sensible. This leads to what Rancière calls 'dis-identification':

> The aesthetic effect itself is initially an effect of dis-identification. The aesthetic community is a community of dis-identified persons. (Rancière 2009a: 73)

It offers a 'multiplicity of folds and gaps in the fabric of common experience that changes the cartography of the perceptible, the thinkable and the feasible' (2009a: 72).

This gives to the art image a different kind of effect from the one associated with critique and 'critical art'. There, Rancière maintains, it was a matter of the image forcing the viewer to confront reality, or a part of reality that they did not want to see. The political collage juxtaposed visual images of comfortable middle-class life with those of the horrors of war in faraway countries, for example. But this strategy, Rancière says, no longer works and probably never had the effects its authors hoped for.

This is related to Rancière's wider argument, that the association of emancipation (equality) with critique as a kind of 'unmasking' was just an unfortunate entanglement. Critique is a particular kind of epistemic orientation that derives from romanticism, and it has no intrinsic connection with the questions of freedom and equality. Art's image, too, need not be critical, but should aspire to disassociate, to allow us to feel that we are equal interpreters (because we are) and that we are all learning through our experiences (because we are): it should affirm reality by giving us objects structured in accordance with the absence of a distorting or biasing regime of the sensible. Art, he says, 'does not involve an illusion but is a matter of shaping a new body and a new sensorium for oneself' (2009a: 71). It is the form of subjectivation specific to art experience that makes art important. In establishing dissonance and dissensus, art separates us from the sensory regime and makes us aware of our fundamental equality with others. In this way, art 'attends to the social bond' (2009b: 120). This is not about art's 'message', which is why Rancière denies any particular significance to 'critical' modernism. Rather, art's subjectivation concerns the fact that in separating from the sensory regime we become aware that others too are subject to this dissensus, this withdrawal, and that as we each have our own, irreducibly different (and non-specifiable) relation to the artwork, that experience is underscored by our knowing that others too have reached this point. Art's subject is equal.

It is here that we find the decisive difference between art and games. As I have indicated, *Journey* is significant for the purity of its gameplay. I would argue that this is bought at the price of a blunting of the game's representational capacities. This is no cost, however. If the game only offered a smooth simulation with pleasurable forms derived from steering your avatar up and into the clouds of red flags, it would cease to be a game and perhaps become a work of art. The main question would then concern the meaning of the game as a strange opening to the unexpected. Indeed, in eschewing the possibility of in-game death, the designers have taken steps in that direction – it is correspondingly doubtful if *Journey* has as many admirers in the gaming community as it has among cultural critics on the lookout for something new. The game relies, however, on the ludic orientation of its players. The mountain is presented early on as the 'goal' to be attained and, in conformity with Bernard Suits' definition of a game discussed in chapter 2, presents a series of unnecessary obstacles to be overcome if we are to get there. This imposes a specific mind-set, a disposition that, along with knowing the conventions of controller use, positions the game as a game. Moreover, by the end of the game, which takes about two-and-a-half hours, different questions are raised, namely, 'How well did I do?', 'How can I know?' and 'Was this a game?'. Indeed, the question of success or failure is mysteriously re-enforced by the fact that there was no possibility of dying and the gameplay was so pure.

Journey, then, is dissociative in the sense discussed earlier, at least in so far as it is a game. Its most interesting episode, however, concerns the presence of other players. At times, the Playstation network combines your play with that of another player, so that there are two identical characters on the screen. Communication is limited to the playing of musical notes, effected by pressing the circle button on the PS3 controller and by dancing around one another. Players can sing in concert and help one another, perhaps by demonstrating the correct way to go, or they can deliberately mislead and even knock other players off course. The way that gameplay is articulated to social connection here is, perhaps, the very antithesis of MMPGs, because the pleasures of play and form are clearly prioritized over communication and the establishment of relationships. There is no sense of attachment to the other, but there is a certain charm in knowing that behind the other character there is another person also on their journey. The play of musical notes back and forth is amusing and so there is scope here for some kind of sentiment to inform the relationship, but the enforced lack of communication and the emphasis on gameplay actually prevent this from escalating into anything more deceptive. In this regard, *Journey* lets us play in the interstices between social points. Its singular encounters of variable significance, all of them inherently transient and resistant to strong narrative investments, create what Nicholas Bourriaud, in his study of contemporary art, calls 'relational microterritories' that 'fill in the cracks in the social bond' (2002: 53). Always in the background, and after we have played the game, is awareness of the other as engaged in the same play and as wondering about us.

Games, then, do present the possibility of dis-identification from the dominant distribution of sensible experience. Viewed in terms of this idea of the aesthetic, I think we can usefully locate the political ambivalence of computer games in terms of three relevant ideas. The first concerns the distinctive role of humour in games and corresponds to the Bergsonian laugh or joke. The second is the relationship of togetherness and aloneness that characterizes our participation in them. The third concerns the role of the childish and of rules.

As we have seen, games are 'fun' in the sense that they promote laughter. People laugh out loud at games in a way that is rare in art galleries. Here we see the consequence of a release of embodied tension associated with the concentrated nature of gameplay as a kind of focused performance. The other effect is that of a kind of technical obtrusion: we become aware that the game, whose 'illusion' has lost its hold on us and no longer rules our activity, is merely a computer program. At this point, we may fall out of the game, perhaps with a feeling of irritation. Either of these outcomes may have the further consequence of leading us to question the value of play with the game. As Henri Bergson (2008 [1940]) says of the laugh, it has a disciplinary function. When our behaviour is most rehearsed and well learned, then our performance may take on a kind of gravity that serves us well most of the time. But when our adherence to the rules of such performances is inappropriate, perhaps because the context has shifted, then we become ridiculous. Bergson says that we are left hanging over a void. He writes,

> The victim . . . of a practical joke is in a position similar to that of a runner who falls, – he is comic for the same reason. The laughable element in both cases consists of a certain *mechanical inelasticity*, just where one would expect to find the wide-awake adaptability and the living pliableness of a human being. (Bergson 2008: 13. Emphasis in original)

These moments in gameplay usually correspond to those of defeat and the appearance of 'game over' on our screens. As we recognize the mechanical in our own behaviour, so we also see it in the game. These moments, which are central to most experience of computer gameplay and almost definitive for its aesthetic, are the ones in which we feel silly and childish, in which our play comes to resemble work and our virtuosity comes to seem like little more than operating a piece of machinery.

There is something cynical about this corrective laughter. It resides in the fact that having encountered a form of dissensus – our expectations have been thwarted in some way, or we have miscalculated in our assessment of the game's intrigue – we do not thereby discover a space for reflection. It is possible that we ask ourselves what other people might have done, but it is more likely that we apply ourselves to repeating the performance only getting it 'right' by doing it 'better'. In this way, the opening created by the game is quickly closed down again by its logic, which is primarily agonistic, or competitive. In our efforts to repeat and correct our performance, then, we focus on getting the moves right and open up a greater distance from the game as a locus of meaningful experience. Our play actually corrodes the game's narrative and characters rather than leading us to stronger feelings of engagement or identification with them. In order to succeed at playing the game, we detach ourselves further from it. But this separation of one order of sense from another is not emancipatory because it only leads to more concentrated and intense performance of actions that become less and less meaningful. We progressively see through the things that made us play with the game but we do not break with it, unless we are bored, in which case withdrawal too is a restoration: a return to the dominant kind of sensible experience.

This brings us to a second set of observations on the aesthetics of engagement with computer games. Games are more structured than artworks by rules that must be learned if we are to play them. This is not determined by the raw materials: play, of an aesthetic variety, is possible with computers; in fact, I have already suggested that such play arises from a natural human disposition, while gameplay is a cultural construct. Games combine play that is determined by the rules in the sense of procedures that must be undergone if we are to 'get anywhere' with free play – those moments when we find our expectations are challenged or undermined in some way. As I suggested above, this defines the dissensus of gaming. However, the result is not an egalitarian subjectivation. Unlike art, gaming is not open to all, or even (which is the same thing) to anyone with an imagination. The primary condition for enjoyment of a game involves no egalitarian assumption corresponding to 'being together by being apart'. As we have seen, those who practise the activity often consciously exclude those they view as ineligible, and gaming culture rests on the idea that some people will be more skilful than others and 'beat' them. This competitive attitude towards others rests on an idea of their irreducible inferiority and not their equality.

The third way of framing gaming's aesthetic dissensus is in terms of the relation of embodied gamer *habitus* to childishness and play. Games offer an experience of embodied learning that, in its open-ended plasticity and susceptibility to constant innovation, is perhaps inherently aesthetic. James Paul Gee describes the same dynamic as outlined by Nielsen, of habituation – naturalization – decoupling – re-habituation, as exploration, automation, adaptation (Gee 2003: 70). He views these as generic moments common to all 'learning situations'. Playing a game becomes a learning experience through the addition of what Gee calls 'embodied understanding', in which players probe, hypothesize, reprobe and think (2003: 91). The patterns they identify in the behaviour of the game object become meaningful as they acquire familiarity and such procedures are the basis of all learning. For this model to work, however, the message of the game's interface – its symbolic dimension – has to cohere with the embodied and ludic dimensions of playing it. Gee argues that games always have a 'semiotic domain', which is a meaningful environment projected by the game's interface that motivates and organizes play. In computer gameplay, he argues, 'we always learn something. And that something is always connected to some semiotic domain or other' (Gee 2003: 22).

For him, these processes are exemplary of critical thinking. Writing in the early years of this century, he argues that increasingly, 'games . . . are crafted in ways that encourage and facilitate active and critical learning' (2003: 46). As people master skills in a game, Gee argues, they must also engage with what the game is about. There is no way for me to master the shotgun in *Resident Evil 4* (2005) without knowing that it has to be found in such and such a place, or that I have enough room in my case to carry it. I will also learn that two shots are not enough to kill the giant mutant frogs that burst through the ground floor windows of the deserted mansion. Failure to learn in this way will be consequential for my performance:

> Learning how to operate the controls of a computer game outside any understanding of the meaningful activities the controls are used to accomplish in the virtual world of the game and outside one's own goals in that world leads, in a shooter game or a realistic military game, for example, to a quick demise (and, thus, not all that much practice, save at dying again and again). In my view, the same is true – metaphorically speaking – in school. (Gee 2003: 69)

However, we can turn this argument on its head. One function of 'gameplay' as a rhetorical strategy constitutive of 'authentic' gaming has been, as we have seen, precisely to stress that concern with character, storyline and other meaningful parts of the semiotic domain is a bit 'soft' and not the real substance of the activity. Gee is surely correct that some semiotic domain is essential, as few games are really abstract in the way that *Tetris* (1984) is, for example. The point, however, is that understanding a game's fiction, how its parts, scenes and themes hang together in a meaningfully rich sense, seems not to be as important as being able to make the game object do things and to extract certain sensations and experiences from it. The issue is not whether a connection always exists between the play and the semiotic meaning, but rather what kind of a connection it is. Analysis that prioritizes the dissociative character of gameplay suggests that critical reflection guided by meanings cued by one's embodied situation 'in' the game is not as important as Gee suggests. Rather, player embodiment is more complex than this and, as the discussion above has suggested, the embodied pleasures of play are central to player enjoyment and function in ways that can be quite independent of the rest of the game object.

Jonas Linderoth (2009) points out that a 'critical approach' on the part of players could be an effect of specific kinds of game design, namely, those that articulate players' motivations to the acquisitions of skills and a deeper understanding of the game world (understood as a fictional construct). However, this kind of design is by no means universal, as the practice of grinding in some MMPGs, discussed in the previous chapter, shows (there players can advance their avatars merely by 'being' in the game and repeating unskilful procedures). Linderoth's point is that while all games require players to become involved and so create the appearance they (the players) are learning something, this can be misleading. Upgrading an avatar 'can be satisfactory in the same way as discovering that you have become better at some skill', but this is, in fact, 'illusory success' (2009: 17), not unlike 'giving someone on a diet a set of scales that showed weight loss without the person actually losing any weight' (Linderoth 2009: 170).

The kind of learning that is essential to art does not concern its messages but rather alterations we perpetrate upon ourselves through our engagement with it, changes that result in a new sense of what is possible. In so far as they require us to perform non-habituated actions to secure unexpected and unanticipated effects, games too can be part of an aesthetic adventure. Whether gaming's aesthetics can have wider, political consequences in the sense of maintaining curiosity as a subjective trait, as against simply integrating people more effectively into a paranoid rat-race, is perhaps an open question. What is clear, however, is that this aesthetic level of analysis is the correct way to investigate computer games in context. Games use their own methods of superimposition to create aesthetic affect. Far from offering ever better simulations, they constantly invite us to play with the strength of their illusion. Repeatedly, it turns out that games do not feel the way we think they will; that we have to do something unexpected with our hands or bodies in order to achieve a result; that that result becomes detached from the meaningful context in which we first encountered it as a goal, and that it becomes a source of mysteriously empty satisfaction after we have repeated those actions to the point where frustration and boredom almost dislodge our interest. Games are pleasurable because they do all this. And in playing games, it follows, we normally have to maintain a high degree of attentiveness and curiosity, just as we do when we engage art's puzzles.

In this chapter, I have tried to show that the social and subjective processes with which these states of mind are articulated in gameplay are not those that define art. Viewed as a form of subjective experience, the practice does not have the same emancipatory implications. We do not find ourselves to be equal with other players, but rather compete with them to perform tasks better, even though we lack a clear sense of the value of those tasks or the significance of victory. In this book, I have tried to show that the preoccupation with making games something more than games is in fact constitutive for the medium. This is to say, as computer gaming culture has grown in confidence and become more mainstream, it has still not managed to secure complete confidence in its own legitimacy as a 'pastime' with intrinsic value. As the comments cited above from the contemporary game press indicate, there is still a question mark over the activity. My proposition is that this residual doubt is in fact constitutive for computer games: in its absence we are no longer talking about a computer game, or gameplay, but have moved on to something else.

It is no easy matter to fathom the political implications of such a cultural practice. The comparison with art is surely the best place to start because of the structural or formal correspondences identified here. Stirring our curiosity and triggering an attentive state of mind in connection with something that is in essence ambiguous and devoid of purpose is something that is only normally associated with art. The differences concern the sociological positioning of the activity. We might be tempted to say that what dignifies art and gives its *illusio* such assurance is simply that respectable people from the middle and ruling classes like art and are participants in it. But my argument suggests there is more to the contrast in terms of both the inherent, psychological dispositions of the gamer and the relation of these to social positions. It is here, in the analysis of an activity that requires us to be constantly changing habituated physiognomic dispositions and a distorted social imaginary that accompanies that activity that we can begin to assess what the real significance of the new medium might be.

Notes

Introduction

1 Among the most important contributions are the works by Garry Crawford (2011), Aphra Kerr (2006), T.L. Taylor (2006, 2012), Mia Consalvo (2008) and Nick Dyer-Witherford and Greg de Peuter (2009). Williams (n.d., 2003) has made the first steps in developing a social history of computer games, while Frans Mäyrä's (2008, 2010) work lays due stress on their social and cultural dimension.

2 The original use of the phrase 'social imaginary' in this context is Cornelius Castoriadis (1987), in his *The Imaginary Institution of Society*, originally published in 1975. My use of the idea is also informed by Jean Duvignaud's (1972) definition in his study of the sociology of art.

Chapter 1: Computer Games in Social Theory

1 In this book, I follow the conventions of ordinary speech by including all games played on or with a digital device under the heading of 'computer games'. It is easier and more felicitous to follow the common usage in this way and to note when specific arguments apply to only some kinds of game and platform than to follow the alternative course, which would probably be to refer to 'digital games'. The latter phrase has the benefit of consistency, although in the case of pervasive games even it is occasionally anomalous, but fidelity to the 'ordinary language' option makes for a more accessible and, hopefully, more user-friendly text.

2 For further discussions, see Arceneaux and Weiss (2010), Van Dijck (2011), Jones (2011), Marwick and Boyd (2011) and Murthy (2011). I return to this issue in chapter 5.

3 Duvignaud (1972) uses the term 'manna' to describe the same concept.

4 This definition is very similar to the one in Jacques Rancière's (2009a) *The Emancipated Spectator*, when he describes 'the point where the *as if* of the community constructed by aesthetic experience meets the *as if* at play in social emancipation' (2009: 70). This play is a 'capacity of anyone whatsoever' to construct new capacities and contribute to the re-shaping of ways of being together in a community. The idea traces back to Immanuel Kant (1960) and Friedrich von Schiller (2008), for whom the imagination plays an active role synthesizing the manifold data of the world into a coherent, uniform experience. This active role of imagination always involves what Schiller calls the 'play instinct' (2008: 28) and, according to him, through play each human subject 'gives reality to the virtuality he bears in him' (2008: 25). These ideas were a crucial reference point for eighteenth-century thinking about equality and democracy.

5 Boltanski and Chiapello (2005: 371) argue that insecurity of this kind is the new form taken by exploitation in networked capitalism.

6 There is a kind of hysteresis, or reverse causation, in operation here, since gaming contributes to the development and spread of this *habitus* in the first place, as I will discuss further in chapter 3.

7 Although Neville already noticed that 'The movement's essential anti-work, pro-play ethic explains why – for all the New Left's braying flirtation with the working class – the affair rarely blossoms into marriage. It is a phony courtship' (1971: 207).

8 The book has been translated into English and was published by Penguin in 2007 under the title *Train Your Brain: 60 Days to a Better Brain* (Kawashima 2007).

9 It is worth noting that some of Kawashima's theories are controversial within the brain science community. Some brain specialists think that the tests, including the Sudoku puzzles, just make you better at doing the tests and question the validity of the claim that this improvement corresponds to having a more youthful or even healthier brain.

10 'There is a problem we will have with a new generation of children – who play computer games – that we have never seen before. The implications are very serious for an increasingly violent society and these students will be doing more and more bad things if they are playing games and not doing other things like reading aloud or learning arithmetic' (*Observer*, 19 August 2001).

11 According to a survey by *New Scientist* magazine, brain training is unlikely to be harmful and there is some evidence to show it

causes improvement in certain specific cognitive functions. Curiously, however, its benefits are most strongly established in connection with remedial therapies for early-stage schizophrenia and other serious mental health conditions with a neuro-physical basis. The gains for people who are free of such problems are unproven: 'Unfortunately for the wannabe genius, there are no simple answers. While there is no shortage of studies suggesting that some cognitive functions can be trained, the link between most of these programs and a better-performing brain is still unproven' (*New Scientist* 2008: 27).

12 Jonas Linderoth (2009) makes a similar point about educational games in a wider sense, which he says make people feel as if teaching and learning are happening even when there is little evidence that this is the case. I discuss this further in chapter 6.

13 This clinging is literal in the case of the DS, which we tend to carry around with us and use in our spare moments. In contrast, the newspaper containing the astrology column is something we might leave behind on the train for someone else to enjoy.

14 This is the positive and enduring presence of gamers and gaming culture that tends to get overlooked by Dyer-Witheford and de Peuter (2009), for whom gamers appear only as a source of energy for the games industry and never as an autonomous factor active in shaping corporate products.

15 Žižek (2009: 71) associates the fetishistic attitude with what he calls a 'permissive cynicism' – anything goes because nothing is consequential.

Chapter 2: Lineages of the Computer Game

1 I first mooted the idea of a playful orientation as an anthropological constant relevant to the study of computer games in Kirkpatrick (2002). It is well supported by the work of Brian Sutton-Smith (2001) and others.

2 As we have seen, though, play is also fundamental to the radical imaginary; the human capacity to re-think and alter social realities.

3 Geoff King and Tanya Krzywinska (2006) try to define a computer game as an amalgam of elements, including gameplay, which might change over time while preserving the designation 'game'. I do not consider this plausible either as a definition or as a methodological strategy.

4 In reality, play is an activity that people engage in throughout the life course. Göncü and Perone (2005) refer to activities like improvised theatre and musical performance to show that play is essential to exploring new inner spaces, to learning from lived experience and even to building community with others.

5 The Nazis were contradictory in their attitude towards arcade and slot machines, which were technically illegal during most of their time in power but often encouraged in practice (Costa 1988: 73), reflecting the Nazis' connections with organized crime and their disregard for consistency in law.

6 'Modded' is a gamer term meaning 'modified'. 'Mods' are game programs produced by gamers' re-working of commercial products and they usually involve changes to the appearance of characters and environments that leave the underlying game architecture and ludic structures unaffected.

7 The controller actually registered electrical impulses generated by tiny muscle movements on the player's forehead.

8 What I call 'folk technology' (Kirkpatrick 2004) is part of the philosophical anthropology mentioned at the end of the last chapter in connection with Boltanski's discussion of footholds for critique.

9 Animals have played computer games: see the papers by Hanna Wirman on the ludus animalis blog: http://ludusanimalis. blogspot.uk/p/touch-project.html.

10 The Altair 8800 was made by Micro Instrumentation Telemetry Systems in Autumn 1974 (Abbate 1999: 138) and marketed through *Popular Electronics* magazine the following year.

11 Freiberger and Swaine point out that the fact games were written in machine code was also a factor. The first micro-computers had very limited memory and so could not support higher-level programming languages. These things conspired to ensure that most people's first encounter with a computer in the 1970s was with a game (Freiberger and Swaine 1984: 132).

12 '[T]he difference between "console" and "game" did not exist yet: all possible games . . . were programmed in the hardware itself' (Malliet and de Meyer 2005: 26).

13 Dmitri Williams writes that Magnavox 'marketed their machine as the new electronic hearth' (Williams n.d.: 3).

14 Their argument is heavily reliant on the theoretical and historical perspective offered by Michael Hardt and Toni Negri (2000).

15 Melanie Swalwell cites research indicating that 60 per cent of software produced for home computers at this time was games

programs, but points out that it is unclear where the games were produced and for which marketplace (Swalwell 2012).

16 Buruma writes that Japanese culture was dominated by a series of fads at this time (1984), so it would have been important to counter this perception as applying to games.

17 This is the context for proper evaluation of Williams' claim that 'games preceded computers at every stage of adoption' of digital technology (n.d.: 5). This statement is correct, but it does not follow that home gaming machines were 'stepping stones to the more complex and powerful world of home computers' (n.d.: 5) because outside the US, games arrived first *with* computers.

18 Realizing Marcuse's vision of a new technology, designed by a new, benign social elite. Marcuse believed that modern technology had the capacity to assign a directing function to the 'free play of thought and imagination' (1964: 234), but this required an aesthetic reform of technology, to translate 'the adventures of the mind into the adventures of technology'.

19 According to Abbate, it was ARPANET's superior funding that ensured it would replace the other networks springing up at this time: 'Though the Internet originated in the United States, it did not simply spread from the United States to the rest of the world. Rather, its global reach resulted from the convergence of many streams of network development' (Abbate 1999: 209). In the UK, people played adventure-style games on networks like the Micro-Net 800, for example.

Chapter 3: The Formation of Gaming Culture

1 This is not to say that people would not have played with computers. If it is true that people work from a relatively fixed repertoire of predispositions that includes play, then computers are the kind of object that will accommodate that orientation; see Kirkpatrick (2002, 2004), Himanen (2002).

2 'Avoid missing ball for high score' (Newman and Simons 2007: 154).

3 Tom Lean (2004) mentions earlier home computing projects, including a computer for the kitchen, but these were one-off hobbyist experiments rather than serious commercial ventures.

4 I am indebted to Melanie Swalwell for discussion of the reception of the magazines in New Zealand and Australia, and to Petri Saarikoski, Jakko Suominen, Veli-Matti Karhulahti, and Christian

Ulrik Andersen for discussions of magazines in the Scandinavian contexts.

5 As Consalvo argues, the magazines taught their young readers 'how to play and what to expect from games' (Consalvo 2008: 25), so that, 'before they can even pick up a controller, their expectations are shaped to some degree about what to expect and what it means to play a game' (Consalvo 2008: 176). Kline et al. also note the importance of game magazines, writing that '*Nintendo Power* played a central role in inventing a game subculture with its own semi-clandestine love of codes, secrets and expertise, a subculture that was at once a reliable market for Nintendo products and a source of information about the changing tastes of gamers' (Kline, Dyer-Witheford and de Peuter 2003: 121).

6 *Commodore User* was conceived by Commodore corporation as part of their marketing (Bagnall 2010).

7 As late as 1989, Nintendo were still trying to convince 'adults to take the Famicom [Japanese forerunner of the NES] seriously enough to use it for stockbroking and banking' (Scheff 1993: 78).

8 The tentative character of these categories, and the novelty of the thinking behind them is reinforced by the fact that four different categories are mooted elsewhere (p. 33) in the same issue of the magazine, namely, action, graphics, addiction and theme.

9 Espen Aarseth has pointed out to me that a similar move occurred within cyber-punk communities at this time, to distance cyber-punks and their cool fictions from mainstream technophiles.

10 In contrast, a review in CVG 2, December 1981, states that 'the best players' of Asteroids 'learn to use the thrust', without importing or invoking any of these wider connotations.

11 Gamer *habitus* acquires a distinctively masculine form in the course of the transformation described here, which in a sense rests upon the move through the icon-based control techniques discussed above to the Nintendo NES and its controller. In this move gaming culture closes around consoles, which is probably an important reason PC gaming retains its appeal for female players (Royse et al. 2007). According to Bourdieu's (2001) analysis of masculine domination, this is precisely the way that gender works through *habitus*. The 'manly man' or the 'womanly woman' are 'social artifacts' produced through a kind of deep dressage that 'concerns every part of the body' (Bourdieu 2001, pp. 23, 27). Bourdieu argues that over much of human history and across many different cultures, there have been observable differences in the ways that men and women comport themselves. I have

suggested that the rules of motion introduced by the *Wii*-mote make it more appealing to women (Kirkpatrick 2011: 131–2).

12 'To be honest, I don't get many girls writing in. I don't know why. If you're a female reader, put down your knitting or crocheting and write and tell me what your views are on the computer industry, or forever remain silent' (CVG, August 1988).

13 In her 'Communities of Play' (2009), Celia Pearce describes a group of players who responded to the closure of their game by forming a diaspora community, while Jenkins (1992, 2006a, 2006b) studies similar episodes in the lives of fans of TV shows. Van Zoonen (2005) reads overt political significance into these kinds of event but her analysis misses the thinness I am highlighting here and so overstates their significance.

14 For further discussion of this issue, see Sarre (2010) and Plowman et al. (2010) as well as the works by Aarsand et al. (2007, 2009).

15 'Cool is now revered as a quality every product tries to be and every child needs to have regardless of age' (Hill 2011: 353).

CHAPTER 4: TECHNOLOGY AND POWER

1 McGonigal (2011) cites an industry figure of US$68 billion.

2 Kline et al. suggest that Nintendo's success in reviving the industry was attributable to a $30 million advertising campaign aimed at convincing people their new games were different from the ones that had disappointed American consumers a few years earlier. Here and elsewhere they tend to reduce the success of games to advertising budgets, neglecting the autonomous effects of gaming as a cultural field.

3 Called the Sega Genesis in the US.

4 Aphra Kerr points out that consoles were always dominant in Japan, accounting for 94 per cent of games sold, while in the US the figure is 80 per cent. The European market remains more attached to PC gaming (consoles accounting for just 55 per cent of sales), although this now seems to be changing (Kerr 2006: 53; De Prato et al. 2010), with a rise in the proportion of games sold for play on mobile devices.

5 1994 was an important year in the history of computing. The PC games *Myst* and *Doom* were both popular in that year and PC sales reached over a million for the first time in the US (Kline et al. 2003: 157). It was also the year the World Wide Web became accessible through the first graphically enabled browser program,

Mosaic (subsequently re-named Netscape). These developments are in part attributable to the rise of gaming and its effects on the wider technical community.

6 The first such concealed programming trick was when Warren Robinett placed his name in flashing letters inside a secret room in the 1978 Atari 2600 version of *Adventure*. The tradition of worker programmers surreptitiously placing items inside commercial software products continues. Modern Mac computers, for instance, contain old arcade games like 'pong' and 'tetris' embedded in their operating systems, accessible using the 'emacs' command in the utilities window. I am grateful to Theodor Araby-Kirkpatrick for showing me this example.

7 Jennifer Johns (2006) suggests that games companies' decision to position offices in Japan, the UK and the US was determined by technology, in particular the presence of different TV technologies, with PAL being used in Europe, NTSC in Asia and the US. This argument overlooks the case of France, which had a different TV standard to everywhere else (Cubitt 2005) but attracted no such attention at this time. It is likely that the decision was driven by a combination of company-specific perceptions of efficiency and the supranational developments discussed by Castells and Sassen.

8 Johns (2006) lists the 2002 value of markets in leisure software by region and shows North American sales at £4.5 billion, European sales at £4.1 billion and Japanese sales at £2.4 billion. In the past decade, as well as growing, the market has shifted towards the East, with the Chinese industry emerging as particularly important for its size and rate of growth (Cao and Downing 2008).

9 Games played on personal computers remain relatively popular in Europe but are in decline everywhere else, having fallen from 17 per cent to 8 per cent of the global market between 2004 and 2009. The decline of PC gaming has been most pronounced in the US, where, as we saw in chapter 3, console games have always been more popular, and it is a tendency that is being reproduced elsewhere, so that the console and hand-held sector now accounts for 60 per cent of game software sales worldwide. It is useful to distinguish single-player PC games from massive multi-player on-line games (MMPGs), which are usually played on a PC but constitute a new and in some ways quite different market.

10 Famicom (family computer) was the Japanese name for the NES.

11 According to cultural historian Ian Buruma, lack of detail especially in the rendering of facial features was a positive value in Japanese aesthetics. Buruma's contemporaneous analysis of

Japanese comic book art at this time highlights contents that would have played well to gaming's field, as defined in chapter 3, especially extreme violence and sex, both involving children and childlike characters (1984: 107–9).

12 Japanese electronics companies were supportive of games development start-ups, while in the US and Europe, games were viewed with suspicion by more 'serious minded' programmers and electronics experts (Aoyama and Izushi 2003: 432).

13 It should be noted that games developers were not shy of approaching media personalities, especially for sports simulators and public events like the 1985 'Soft Aid'. However, these examples show that the positive associations were with sport and popular music, revealing how segmented UK entertainment culture was at the time, which confirms the thesis.

14 This should also be seen in the context of a range of legal challenges to the validity of Nintendo's attempts to monopolize the industry, which forced them to allow developers in the US in particular to make games for Nintendo machines (see Scheff 1993; Kline et al. 2003).

15 It is interesting in this regard to contrast the different ways that games corporations involve themselves in education-related projects. For example, Konami fund 'Computer Entertainment Schools' in Tokyo and Osaka (Aoyama and Izushi 2003: 440), while US corporations tend to pursue links with universities and the military as a way to get additional funding for experimental projects (Dyer-Witheford and de Peuter 2009: 102), although Dyer-Witheford and Sharman do mention more educational investment by Canadian developers in Ontario and British Columbia (2005: 201).

16 Benoît Sokal has explained his move away from games and back to graphic novels in terms that are consistent with this:

> This industry has grown in a monstrous way. What I was able to do 7 or 8 years ago is impossible today. Already, at that time it took a firm of some consequence, more than a hundred people, to work on a game like *Syberia*; but it was, curiously, a project on a human scale. Today game 'authors' of the kind I was are not possible any more. The game world, the landscape, the mechanics have changed, all accompanied by an important inflation in the role of finance. I never wanted to be employed in a business like the one it has become. I am and I remain, before everything, an author. (Picaud 2010; my translation)

17 Much of the commentary on this episode rests on the (false) assumption that violence appeals to teenage boys and that corporations cynically pander to this. I submit that here and in subsequent similar controversies a particular group of teenage boys, equipped with a specific set of cultural skills and preferences, enjoyed making other people uncomfortable with the idea that they were doing something violent. The real pleasure lies in the mismatch of perceptions, in which often only one side is at all knowing.

18 Microsoft have even released a free SDK, Game Studio Express, to allow players to make their own games for the X-Box (Deuze et al. 2007: 340).

19 On occasion, these proprietary claims are quite shocking in their reach. Purchasers of the Nintendo 3DS, for example, released in 2011, are also, whether they like it or not, signatories to an agreement that means their machine will be subject to updates downloaded through wireless connection at any time. These updates will disable any modded software introduced by the Wiikey chip, mentioned above, or any other 'unauthorised peripherals'. But more insidious than any of this, the EULA states that all user-generated content, which includes messages and photos created using the machine's communication and camera functions, belongs to Nintendo (Doctorow 2011).

Chapter 5: The Phenakisticon

1 Meaning, here, turns on assessment of the significance to us of the relationships formed in terms of how they feature in our attempts at self-understanding and their usefulness when trying to form a conception of the social whole in which those relationships play a part.

2 Castronova defines a synthetic world as follows: 'any computer-generated physical space, represented graphically in three dimensions, that can be experienced by many people at once' (2005: 22).

3 It follows that the I, in this sense, is the necessary opening to the radical imaginary and the possibility of establishing new practices and discourses through which to make sense of the world and which form the basis of participation in it.

4 The distinction of the inner 'I' from the 'me', which is the sense I have of myself based on how others treat me and the recognition they afford me, is taken from Herbert Mead's (1987 [1934]) *Mind, Self and Society*.

5 Kirkpatrick (2010) and others (e.g. Arcenaux and Weiss 2010) refer to 'ambient intimacy' associated with Facebook and other new social media.

6 Journalist Julian Dibbell described an incident which took place in LambdaMOO, during which one player used a hacking program to take control of another's character and make it appear as if they were engaging in sexual acts in the public space of the game environment.

7 Perhaps significantly, RPers use chat channels less than other players (Williams et al. 2011: 191).

8 Lash and Lury (2007: 142) use an analogy with 'junk', or drug, addiction in their account of all 'virtual' commodities.

9 This attitude resonates with Juul's (2010) identification of an increasingly 'casual' gaming ethos.

10 Honneth writes that 'the experience of being socially esteemed is accompanied by a felt confidence that one's achievements or abilities will be recognized as "valuable" by other members of society' (Honneth 1995: 128).

11 'Persons can feel themselves to be "valuable" only when they know themselves to be recognized for accomplishments that they precisely do not share with others' (Honneth 1995: 125).

12 Even if players open second and third accounts in which they create new avatars of different types, which we know many players do, this will only be to embrace similar limitations and to be disposed in a different, pre-programmed way in the game. The principle that a chosen body of a given 'type' limits our capacities to act while promoting certain other abilities is thoroughly inscribed in the game and conditions all recognition processes in the game world.

13 Yee reports that 'many users across all age ranges form meaningful relationships in MMORPGs' (Yee 2006: 321) and argues that games incentivize the formation of 'strong ties' (Yee 2006: 322).

14 At the time of writing, a typical MMPG subscription is around £12.50 per month.

15 Print's implication in what was to become enlightenment was not a straightforward matter of the dissemination of reliable information. Much of what was printed was mystical and trashy, much as now. What print transformed was the methodology of knowledge production. Eisenstein (1983) refers to a new scientific culture based on intensive 'cross reference' made possible by the availability of reliable, printed sources.

16 The return on gold-farmed goods to producers has been estimated to be comparable to that of coffee, a notable 'third world export',

and in fact a higher proportion of the return gets back to the labourers who produce it (Lehdonvirto and Ernkvist 2011).

17 This describes a kind of collapse, or diffusion, of the energies in gaming's field, which correlates to the critique of the magic circle of play, mounted by T.L. Taylor and other MMPG scholars. Once play is with sociality rather than productive of it, its energies are dissipated and the field loses its charge.

CHAPTER 6: AESTHETICS AND POLITICS

1 The BBFC research concludes that 'with emphatic exceptions, storylines appear to be a relatively weak element in the overall appeal of games' (BBFC 2005: 10). This research also confirms the paradox that players are both intensely engaged by play processes and curiously disinterested in the practice, easily switching to other activities (cf. Fromme 2003).

2 Historical distance and technological changes make this point very clear: it is almost inconceivable that anyone might be aroused by a text-based adventure game with puzzles. In fact, it was already clear to the game's 1980s reviewers.

3 Play with games has completely different physiognomic effects from engagement with other media, including watching things on even very bright screens (Higuchi et al. 2005).

4 Shinkle says that the Wii makes games more 'fun', but this is a personal judgement. As I have argued here and elsewhere (Kirkpatrick 2011), the fun and laughter element of games was always about embodied tensions and their release. I agree that the fun element is more obvious when the tensions released are in a body falling through living room space, as against a hand wrapped around a controller.

5 Velli-Matti Karhulahti (2012) points out that gaming is unusual in the history of expressive performance in that much of the time players perform only for their own pleasure.

6 This does not mean we should not try. In Kirkpatrick (2011), I have tried to clarify gameplay as a concept in the philosophical analysis of contemporary experiences of aesthetic form.

7 This is grasped within game theory by the idea of Ilinx, defined by Roger Caillois as 'an attempt to momentarily destroy the stability of perception and inflict a kind of voluptuous panic on an otherwise lucid mind' (1958: 23).

8 Failure to understand this leads to literalist interpretations of game content, which treat games as if they were films. The

principle that play distantiates, along with the fact that parents and other authority figures only watch games, probably explains their tendency to 'extreme' graphic representations. Play has done this kind of distancing work more in some cultural contexts than others (see Kirkpatrick 2011: 175). According to Buruma, 'In Japan even the most horrifying violence, as long as it is not real, can be judged purely aesthetically' (1984: 223), as long as it has an element of play.

9 Play with computer games has implications for the status of childhood, implicit in Shigeru Miyamoto's comment that any game he was designing 'is not for children, it is for me. It is for the adult that still has the character of the child' (cited in Scheff 1993: 51).

10 Rancière's attack on Boltanski, in *The Emancipated Spectator* (2009a: 34), accuses the latter of having a 'flimsy conceptual framework' but this seems ill-judged. As far as the crisis of traditional critique is concerned, their analyses are quite close. Boltanski, rightly in my view, insists that the moment of dissonance itself *is* a kind of critique, writing that 'the slightest gap between reality and world is the equivalent of a critique' (2011: 98).

References

Aarsand, P.A. (2007) 'Computer and video games in family life: the digital divide as a resource in intergenerational interactions', Childhood 14(2), 235–56.

Aarsand, P.A. and Aronsson, K. (2009) 'Gaming and territorial negotiations in family life', Childhood 16(4), 497–517.

Aarseth, E. (2006) 'The culture and business of cross-media production', Popular Communications 4(3), 203–11.

Abbate, J. (1999) Inventing the Internet. Cambridge, MA: MIT Press.

Adams, M. (2007) Self and Social Change. London: Sage.

Adorno, T.W. (1994) The Stars Down to Earth and Other Essays on the Irrational in Culture. London: Routledge.

Adorno, T.W. (2002) Aesthetic Theory. London: Continuum.

Adorno, T.W. and Horkheimer, M. (1997) Dialectic of Enlightenment. London: Verso.

Andersen, C.U. (2012) 'Making games with software: the logic of sensation in Spacewar!', in P. Krejewski (ed.) WRO 2011, Alternative new catalog, Wroclaw: WRO foundation for media art, pp. 25–31.

Anderson, B. (1985) Imagined Communities. London: Verso.

Aoyama, Y. and Izushi, H. (2003) 'Hardware gimmick or cultural innovation? Technological, cultural and social foundations of the Japanese video game industry', Research Policy 32(3), 423–44.

Appadurai, A. (ed.) (1988) The Social Life of Things: Commodities in Cultural Perspective. Cambridge: Cambridge University Press.

Arceneaux, N. and Weiss, A.S. (2010) 'Seems stupid until you try it: press coverage of Twitter, 2006–9', New Media & Society 12(8), 1262–79.

Bagnall, B. (2010) Commodore: A Company on the Edge. Winnipeg: Variant Books.

Behrenshausen, B. (2007) 'Toward a (kin)aesthetic of video gaming: the case of Dance Dance Revolution', Games and Culture 2(4), 335–54.

Bennerstedt, U. and Ivarsson, J. (2010) 'Knowing the way: managing epistemic topologies in virtual game worlds', *Computer Supported Cooperative Work* 19(2), 201–30.

Bergson, H. (2008 [1940]) *Laughter: An Essay on the Meaning of the Comic*. Rockville, MD: Arc Manor.

Bijker, W., Hughes, T. and Pinch, T. (1989) *The Social Construction of Technological Systems: New Directions in the Sociology and History of Technology*. Cambridge, MA: MIT Press.

Boltanski, L. (2011) *On Critique: A Sociology of Emancipation*. Cambridge: Polity.

Boltanski, L. and Chiapello, E. (2005) *The New Spirit of Capitalism*. London: Verso.

Bourdieu, P. (1995) *The Field of Cultural Production*. Cambridge: Polity.

Bourdieu, P. (2001) *Masculine Domination*. Cambridge: Polity.

Bourdieu, P. (2009 [1996]) *The Rules of Art*. Cambridge: Polity.

Bourriaud, N. (2002) *Relational Aesthetics*. Dijon: Les presses du réel.

Buruma, I. (1984) *A Japanese Mirror: Heroes and Villains of Japanese Culture*. London: Penguin.

Caillois, R. (1958) *Man, Play and Games*. Paris: Gallimard.

Cao, Y. and Downing, J. (2008) 'The realities of virtual play: video games and their industry in China', *Media, Culture & Society* 30(4), 515–29.

Carstens, A. and Beck, J. (2005) 'Get ready for the gamer generation', *Techtrends* 49(3), 22–5.

Castells, M. (1996) *The Rise of the Network Society*. Oxford: Blackwell.

Castoriadis, C. (1987) *The Imaginary Institution of Society*. Cambridge: Polity Press.

Castronova, E. (2005) *Synthetic Worlds: The Business and Culture of Online Games*. Chicago, IL: Chicago University Press.

Ceruzzi, P. (2000) *A History of Modern Computing*. Cambridge, MA: MIT Press.

Chanan, M. (1996) *The Dream That Kicks: The Prehistory and Early Years of Cinema in Britain*. London: Routledge.

Chandler, A. (1996) 'The changing definition and image of hackers in popular discourse', *International Journal of the Sociology of Law* 24(2), 229–51.

Comment, B. (2002) *The Panorama*. London: Reaktion Books.

Consalvo, M. (2006) 'Console video games and global corporations: creating a hybrid culture', *New Media and Society* 8(1), 117–37.

Consalvo, M. (2008) *Cheating in Video Games*. Cambridge, MA: MIT Press.

Costa, N. (1988) *Automatic Pleasures: The History of the Coin Machine*. London: Bath Press.

Crabtree, G. (2010) 'Playing at war: games technologies and British military imaginings, 1870–2010', PhD thesis, University of Manchester.

Crary, J. (1993) Techniques of the Observer: On Vision and Modernity in the Nineteenth Century. Cambridge, MA: MIT Press.

Crawford, G. (2006) 'The cult of Champ Man: the culture and pleasures of championship manager/football manager gamers', Information, Communication & Society 9(4), 496–514.

Crawford, G. (2011) Video Gamers. London: Routledge.

Crewe, L. and Collins, P. (2006) 'Commodifying children: fashion, space and the production of the profitable child', Environment and Planning A 38(1), 7–24.

Crogan, P. (2010) 'The Nintendo Wii, virtualisation and gestural analogics', Culture Machine 11, 82–101.

Crogan, P. (2012) Gemplay Mode. Minneapolis, MN: University of Minnesota Press.

Crouch, C. (2011) The Strange Non-Death of Neoliberalism. Cambridge: Polity.

David, M. (2010) Peer to Peer and the Music Industry: The Criminalization of Sharing. London: Sage.

De Prato, G., Frijoo, C., Nepelski, D., Bogdanowicz, M. and Simon, J.P. (2010) 'Born digital/grown digital: assessing the future competitiveness of the EU video games software industry', Seville: European Commission Joint Research Centre/Institute for Prospective Technological Studies.

Deuze, M. (2007) Media Work. Cambridge: Polity.

Deuze, M., Bowen Martin, C. and Allen, C. (2007) 'The professional identity of gameworkers', Convergence 13(4), 335–53.

Dibbell, J. (1991) 'A rape in cyberspace', The Village Voice, 21 December.

Doctorow, C. (2011) 'Nintendo 3DS license: We'll brick your device if we don't like your software choices, you have no privacy, we own your photos', BoingBoing blog: http://boingboing.net/2011/05/17/nintendo-3ds-license.html (accessed June 2011).

Dovey, J. and Kennedy, H. (2006) Game Cultures: Computer Games as New Media. Maidenhead: McGraw-Hill.

Duvignaud, J. (1972) The Sociology of Art. London: Paladin.

Dyer-Witheford, N. and de Peuter, G. (2009) Games of Empire: Global Capitalism and Video Games. Minneapolis, MN: University of Minnesota Press.

Dyer-Witheford, N. and Sharman, Z. (2005) 'The political economy of Canada's video and computer game industry', Canadian Journal of Communication 30(2), 187–210.

Economist (2011) 'The serious business of fun', *Economist*, 10–16 December.

Edge (2008) 'Ever decreasing circles', *Edge: Videogame Culture*, March.

Ehrenreich, B. (2009) *Smile or Die: How Positive Thinking Fooled America and the World*. London: Granta.

Eisenstein, E. (1983) *The Printing Revolution in Early Modern Europe*. Cambridge: Cambridge University Press.

Enticknap, L. (2005) *Moving Image Technology: From Zoetrope to Digital*. London: Wallflower Press.

Farne, R. (2005) 'Pedagogy of play', *Topoi* 24(2), 169–81.

Feenberg, A. (1995) *Alternative Modernity*. Berkeley, CA: University of California Press.

Feenberg, A. (2002) *Transforming Technology*. Oxford: Oxford University Press.

Feenberg, A. (2010) *Between Reason and Experience*. Cambridge, MA: MIT Press

Feenberg, A. and Freedman, J. (2001) *When Poetry Ruled the Streets: The French Events of May 1968*. New York: SUNY Press.

Foucault, M. (1985) *Discipline and Punish: The Birth of the Prison*. London: Peregrine.

Freiberger, P. and Swaine, M. (1984) *Fire in the Valley: The Making of the Personal Computer*. London: McGraw-Hill.

Fromme, J. (2003) 'Computer games as a part of children's culture', *Game Studies* 3(1).

Galloway, A. (2006) *Gaming: Essays on Algorithmic Culture*. Minneapolis, MN: University of Minnesota Press.

Gee, J.P. (2003) *What Video Games Have to Teach Us about Learning and Literacy*. Basingstoke: Palgrave Macmillan.

Golumbia, D. (2009) 'Games without play', *New Literary History* 40(1), 179–204.

Göncü, A. and Perone, A. (2005) 'Pretend play as a life-span activity', *Topoi* 24(2), 137–47.

Gordon, D.R. (1987) 'The electronic panopticon: a case study of the development of the national criminal records system', *Politics & Society* 15(4), 483–511.

Gregersen, A. (2011) 'Genre, technology and embodied interaction: the evolution of digital game genres and motion gaming', *MediaKultur* 51, 94–109.

Habermas, J. (1987) *Knowledge and Human Interests*. Cambridge: Polity.

Habermas, J. (1989) *The Structural Transformation of the Public Sphere*. Cambridge: Polity Press.

References 205

Habermas, J. (1995) *Justification and Application*. Cambridge: Polity.

Habermas, J. (2003) *The Future of Human Nature*. Cambridge: Polity.

Haddon, L. (1988) 'The home computer: the making of a consumer electronic', *Science as Culture* 2, 7–51.

Hafner, K. and Lyon, M. (1996) *Where Wizards Stay Up Late: The Origins of the Internet*. New York: Touchstone.

Hardt, M. and Negri, A. (2000) *Empire*. Cambridge, MA: Harvard University Press.

Hayot, E. and Wesp, E. (2009) 'Towards a critical aesthetic of virtual-world geographies', *Game Studies* 9(1).

Haythornthwaite, C. (2002) 'Strong, weak, and latent ties and the impact of new media', *Information Society* 18(5), 385–401.

Heeks, R. (2010) 'Understanding "gold farming" and real-money trading as the intersection of real and virtual economies', *Journal of Virtual Worlds Research* 2(4).

Heidegger, M. (2002 [1950]) 'The question concerning technology', in R. Scharff and V. Dusek (eds) *Philosophy of Technology: The Technological Condition: An Anthology*. Oxford: Blackwell.

Held, D. (1989) *Introduction to Critical Theory*. Cambridge: Polity.

Higgin, T. (2009) 'Blackless fantasy: the disappearance of race in massively multiplayer online role playing games', *Games and Culture* 4(1), 3–26.

Higuchi, S., Motohashi, Y., Liu, Y. and Maeda, A. (2005) 'Effects of playing a computer game using a bright display on presleep physiological variables, sleep latency, slow wave sleep and REM sleep', in *Journal of Sleep Research* (2005) 14, 267–73.

Hill, J.A. (2011) 'Endangered childhoods: how consumerism is impacting child and youth identity', *Media, Culture & Society* 33(3), 347–62.

Himanen, P. (2002) *The Hacker Ethic and the Spirit of the Information Age*. New York: Random House.

Honneth, A. (2005 [1995]) *The Struggle for Recognition: The Moral Grammar of Social Conflicts*. Cambridge: Polity.

Huhtamo, E. (2005) 'Slots of fun, slots of trouble: an archaeology of arcade gaming', in J. Raessens and J. Goldstein (eds) *Handbook of Computer Game Studies*. Cambridge, MA: MIT Press.

Huizinga, J. (1950) *Homo Ludens: The Play Element in Culture*. Boston, MA: Beacon Press.

Humphreys, S. (2008) 'Ruling the virtual world: governance in massively multiplayer online games', *European Journal of Cultural Studies* 11(2), 149–71.

Humphreys, S. (2009) 'Norrath: new forms, old institutions', *Game Studies* 9(1).

Illich, I. (1971) *Tools for Conviviality*. Harmondsworth: Penguin.

Izushi, H. and Aoyama, Y. (2006) 'Industry evolution and cross-sectoral skill transfers: a comparative analysis of the video game industry in Japan, the United States, and the United Kingdom', *Environment and Planning A* 38(10), 1843–61.

Jansz, J. and Martens, L. (2005) 'Gaming at a LAN event: the social context of playing video games', *New Media & Society* 7(3), 333–55.

Jay, M. (1973) *The Dialectical Imagination: A History of the Frankfurt School and the Institute for Social Research 1931–1950*. Berkeley, CA: University of California Press.

Jenkins, H. (1992) *Textual Poachers: Television Fans and Participatory Culture*. London: Routledge.

Jenkins, H. (2006a) *Fans, Bloggers, and Gamers: Exploring Participatory Culture*. New York: New York University Press.

Jenkins, H. (2006b) *Convergence Culture: Where Old and New Media Collide*. New York: New York University Press.

Johns, J. (2006) 'Video games production networks: value capture, power relations and embeddedness', *Journal of Economic Geography* 6, 151–80.

Johnson, S. (1997) *Interface Culture: How Computers Change the Way We Create and Communicate*. New York: Basic Books.

Jones, G. (2004) *Men of Tomorrow: Geeks, Gangsters and the Birth of the Comic Book*. New York: Basic Books.

Jones, J. (2011) 'Social media and social movements', *International Socialism Journal* 130.

Joyce, M. (ed.) (2010) *Digital Activism Decoded*. New York: International Debate Education Association.

Juul, J. (2010) *A Casual Revolution: Reinventing Video Games and Their Players*. Cambridge, MA: MIT Press.

Kant, I. (1960) *The Critique of Judgement*. Oxford: Clarendon Press.

Karhulahti, V.M. (2012) 'Pissing in the fountain: videogames and expressive performance', *Italian Journal of Game Studies* 1(2).

Kawabata, Y. (1972) *The Master of Go*. New York: Knopf.

Kawashima, R. (2007) *Train Your Brain: 60 Days to a Better Brain*. Harmondsworth: Penguin.

Keen, A.J. (2012) *Digital Vertigo*. London: Constable and Robinson.

Kendrick, L. (2009) 'Games medievalists play: how to make earnest of a game and still enjoy it', *New Literary History* 40(1), 43–61.

Kent, S. (2001) *The Ultimate History of Video Games*. Roseville, CA: Prima Press.

Kerr, A. (2006) *The Business and Culture of Digital Games*. London: Sage.

Kirby, L. (1997) *Parallel Tracks: Railroad and Silent Cinema*. Exeter: University of Exeter Press.

Kirkpatrick, D. (2010) *The Facebook Effect*. London: Virgin Books.

Kirkpatrick, G. (2002) 'The hacker ethic and the spirit of informationalism', *Max Weber Studies* 2(2).

Kirkpatrick, G. (2004) *Critical Technology: A Social Theory of Personal Computing*. Aldershot: Ashgate.

Kirkpatrick, G. (2008) *Technology and Social Power*. Basingstoke: Palgrave Macmillan.

Kirkpatrick, G. (2009) 'Controller, hand, screen: aesthetic form in the computer game', *Games and Culture* 4(2), 127–43.

Kirkpatrick, G. (2011) *Aesthetic Theory and the Video Game*. Manchester: Manchester University Press.

Kirkpatrick, G. (2012) 'Constitutive tensions of gaming's field: UK gaming magazines and the formation of gaming culture, 1981–1995', *Game Studies* 12(1).

Klastrup, E. (2009) 'The worldness of EverQuest: exploring a 21st century fiction', *Game Studies* 9(1).

Kline, S., Dyer-Witheford, N. and de Peuter, G. (2003) *Digital Play*. Ottawa: McQueen-Gill University Press.

Kocurek, C. (2012) 'The agony and the Exidy: a history of video game violence and the legacy of *Death Race*', *Game Studies* 12(1).

Kücklich, J. (2005) 'Precarious playbour: modders and the digital games industry', *Fibreculture Journal* 5.

Kushner, D. (2003) *Masters of Doom*. London: Pantheon.

Lash, S. and Lury, C. (2007) *Global Culture Industry*. Cambridge: Polity.

Lastowka, G. (2009) 'Planes of power: EverQuest as text, game and community', *Game Studies* 9(1).

Latham, M. and Sassen, S. (eds) (2005) *Digital Formations: IT and Digital Structures in the Global Realm*. Princeton, NJ: Princeton University Press.

Latour, B. (2005) *Reassembling the Social: An Introduction to Actor-Network-Theory*. Oxford: Oxford University Press.

Laurel, B. (1995) *Computers as Theatre*. London: Addison-Wesley.

Lean, T. (2004) 'Sinclair computers in the home', unpublished Master's thesis, University of Manchester.

Leary, T. (1990) 'The interpersonal, interactive, interdimensional interface', in B. Laurel (ed.) *The Art of Human–Computer Interface Design*. Cambridge, MA: MIT Press.

Lehdonvirto, V. and Ernkvist, M. (2011) 'Knowledge map of the virtual economy: converting the virtual economy into development potential', International Bank for Reconstruction and Development/The World Bank, available from www.infodev.org (accessed May 2011).

Leino, O.T. (2012) 'Untangling gameplay: an account of experience, activity and materiality within computer game play', in J. Sageng, H. Fossheim and T. Mandt Larsen (eds) The Philosophy of Computer Games. London: Springer.

Levy, S. (1984) Hackers: Heroes of the Computer Revolution. Harmondsworth: Penguin.

Linderoth, J. (2009) 'It is not hard – it just requires having no life: computer games and the illusion of learning', Nordic Journal of Digital Literacy 01, 4–19.

Linderoth, J. and Bennerstadt, U. (2007) 'Living in World of Warcraft: the thoughts and experiences of ten young people', Göteborg University, Department of Education, Swedish Media Council.

Lovink, G. (2008) Zero Comments: Blogging and Critical Internet Culture. London: Routledge.

Lugo, J., Sampson, T. and Lossada, M. (2002) 'Latin America's new cultural industries still play old games: from the banana republic to Donkey Kong', Game Studies 2(2).

Malliet, S. and de Meyer, G. (2005) 'The history of the videogame', in J. Raessens and J. Goldstein (eds) Computer Game Studies Handbook. Cambridge, MA: MIT Press.

Marcuse, H. (1964) One Dimensional Man. London: Ark.

Marcuse, H. (1978) The Aesthetic Dimension. Basingstoke: Macmillan.

Marwick, A.E. and Boyd, D. (2011) 'I tweet honestly, I tweet passionately: Twitter users, context collapse, and the imagined audience', New Media & Society 13(1), 114–33.

Marx, K. (1990) Capital Volume One. London: Penguin.

Mathieson, T. (1997) 'The viewer society: Foucault's "panopticon" revisited', Theoretical Criminology 1(2), 215–34.

Matthews, S.H. (2007) 'A window on the "new" sociology of childhood', Sociology Compass 1(1), 322–34.

Mäyrä, F. (2008) 'Open invitation: mapping global game cultures: issues for a sociocultural study of games and players', European Journal of Cultural Studies 11(2), 249–57.

Mäyrä, F. (2010) An Introduction to Game Studies. London: Sage.

McGonigal, J. (2011) Reality is Broken: Why Games Make Us Better and How They Can Change the World. London: Jonathan Cape.

Mead, G.H. (1987 [1934]) Mind, Self, and Society: From the Standpoint of a Social Behaviorist. Chicago, IL: University of Chicago Press.

Melucci, A. (1996) *The Playing Self: Person and Meaning in the Planetary Society*. Cambridge: Cambridge University Press.

Ming Kow, Y. and Nardi, B. (2009) 'Culture and creativity: WoW modding in China and the US', in W. Sims Bainbridge (ed.) *Online Worlds: Convergence of the Real and the Virtual*. London: Springer.

Montfort, N. and Bogost, I. (2009) *Racing the Beam: The Atari Computing System*. Cambridge, MA: MIT Press.

Morozov, E. (2010) *The Net Delusion: How Not to Liberate the World*. London: Allen Lane.

Mouchart, B. (2003) *La Bande Dessinée*. Paris: Le cavalier bleu.

Murthy, D. (2011) 'Twitter: microphone for the masses?', *Media, Culture & Society* 33(5), 779–89.

Napier, S.J. (2005) *Anime: From Akira to Howl's Moving Castle*. Basingstoke: Palgrave Macmillan.

Negroponte, N. (1995) *Being Digital*. London: Coronet.

Neville, R. (1971) *Playpower*. London: Paladin.

Newman, J. (2004) *Videogames*. London: Routledge.

Newman, J. and Simons, I. (2007) *100 Videogames*. London: BFI Screen Guides.

New Scientist (2008) 'Does brain training work?', *New Scientist*, 12 January.

Nieborg, D.B. and Hermes, J. (2008) 'What is game studies anyway? *European Journal of Cultural Studies* 11(2), 131–46.

Nieborg, D.B. and van der Graaf, S. (2008) 'The mod industries? The industrial logic of non-market game production', *European Journal of Cultural Studies* 11(2), 177–95.

Nielsen, H.S. (2010) 'The computer game as a somatic experience', *Eludamos* 4(1), 25–40.

O'Leary, T. (2002) *Foucault and the Art of Ethics*. London: Continuum.

Paris, M. (2000) *Warrior Nation: Images of War in British Popular Culture 1850–2000*. London: Reaktion Books.

Pearce, C. (2009) *Communities of Play: Emergent Cultures in Multiplayer Games and Virtual Worlds*. Cambridge, MA: MIT Press.

Pfaffenberger, B. (1988) 'The social meaning of the personal computer', *Anthropology Quarterly* 61(1), 39–47.

Picaud, F. (2010) 'Entretien avec Benoît Sokal': www.auracan.com/Interviews/interview.php?auteur=155 (accessed November 2011).

Plowman, L., McPake, J. and Stephen, C. (2010) 'The technologisation of childhood? Young children and technology in the home', *Children and Society* 24(1), 63–74.

Poole, S. (2000) *Trigger Happy: The Inner Life of Video Games*. London: Fourth Estate.

Prax, P. (2012) 'The Gorefiend Emulator', unpublished paper presented to PhD conference, Sandbjerg Gods, May.

Rancière, J. (2009a) *The Emancipated Spectator*. London: Verso.

Rancière, J. (2009b) *Aesthetics and Its Discontents*. Cambridge: Polity.

Rheingold, H. (1997) *Homesteading on the Virtual Frontier*. Reading, MA: Addison-Wesley.

Roe Smith, M. and Marx, G. (eds) (1994) *Does Technology Drive History? The Dilemmas of Determinism*. Cambridge, MA: MIT Press.

Roszack, T. (1968) *The Making of a Counter Culture: Reflections on the Technocratic Society and its Youthful Opposition*. London: Faber & Faber.

Royse, P., Lee, J., Undrahbuyan, B., Hopson, M. and Consalvo, M. (2007) 'Women and games: technologies of the gendered self', *New Media and Society*, 9(4), 555–76.

Ruch, A. (2009) 'World of Warcraft: service or space?', *Game Studies* 9(2).

Ruckenstein, M. (2010) 'Toying with the world: children, virtual pets and the value of mobility', *Childhood* 17(4), 500–13.

Sarre, S. (2010) 'Parental regulation of teenagers' time: processes and meanings', *Childhood* 17(1), 61–75.

Sassen, S. (2006) *Territory, Authority, Rights*. Princeton, NJ: Princeton University Press.

Scheff, D. (1993) *Game Over: How Nintendo Zapped an American Industry, Captured your Dollars and Enslaved your Children*. New York: Random House.

Schiller, F. von (2008) *Letters upon the Aesthetic Education of Man*. Whitefish, MT: Kessinger Publishing.

Selwyn, N. (2002) 'Learning to love the micro: the discursive construction of "educational" computing in the UK, 1979–89', *British Journal of Sociology of Education* 23(3), 427–43.

Selwyn, N. (2003) 'Doing IT for the kids: re-examining children, computers and the information society', *Media, Culture & Society* 25(3), 351–78.

Selwyn, N. (2010) *Schools and Schooling in the Digital Age: A Critical Perspective*. London: Routledge.

Sennett, R. (2006) *The Culture of the New Capitalism*. New Haven, CT: Yale University Press.

Shinkle, E. (2008) 'Video games emotion and the six senses', *Media, Culture & Society* 30(6), 907–15.

Shusterman, R. (2008) *Body Consciousness: A Philosophy of Mindfulness and Somaesthetics*. Cambridge: Cambridge University Press.

Simon, B., Boudreau, K. and Silverman, M. (2009) 'Two players: biography and played sociality in EverQuest', *Game Studies* 9(1).

Sloterdijk, P. (1987) *Critique of Cynical Reason*. Minneapolis, MN: University of Minnesota Press.

Sotamaa, O. (2009) 'The player's game: towards understanding player production among computer game cultures', *PhD thesis*, Finland: University of Tampere.

Stafford, B. (1994) *Artful Science: Enlightenment, Entertainment and the Eclipse of Visual Education*. Cambridge, MA: MIT Press.

Sterling, B. (1992) *The Hacker Crackdown: Law and Order on the Electronic Frontier*. Harmondsworth: Penguin.

Suits, B. (1978) *The Grasshopper: Games, Life and Utopia*. Edinburgh: Edinburgh University Press.

Sutton-Smith, B. (2001) *The Ambiguity of Play*. Cambridge, MA: Harvard University Press.

Swalwell, M. (2012) 'The early micro user: games writing, hardware hacking and the will to mod', Proceedings of Nordic DiGRA.

Tanke, J. (2012) *Jacques Rancière: An Introduction*. London: Acumen.

Taylor, C. (2004) *Modern Social Imaginaries*. Cambridge: Polity.

Taylor, P.A. (1999) *Hackers: Crime in the Digital Sublime*. London: Routledge.

Taylor, T.L. (2006) *Play Between Worlds: Exploring Online Game Culture*. Cambridge, MA: MIT Press.

Taylor, T.L. (2012) *Raising the Stakes: E-sports and the Professionalization of Gaming*. Cambridge, MA: MIT Press.

Thompson, J. (1995) *The Media and Modernity*. Cambridge: Polity.

Tosca, S. (2003) 'Life's a game: play more in the third place', paper presented to Digital Industries Symposium, CRIC, University of Manchester.

Turkle, S. (1995) *Life on the Screen*. London: Schuster and Schuster.

Turkle, S. (2010) *Alone Together: Why We Expect More From Technology and Less From Each Other*. New York: Basic Books.

Turner, F. (2006) *From Counterculture to Cyberculture*. Chicago, IL: Chicago University Press.

Vanard, K. (2011) Soapbox piece on Gamespot web-site: http://uk.gamespot.com/soapbox/index.html (accessed July 2011).

Van Dijck, J. (2009) 'Users like you? Theorizing agency in user-generated content', *Media, Culture & Society* 31(1), 41–58.

Van Dijck, J. (2011) 'Facebook as a tool for producing sociality and connectivity', *Television & New Media* 13(2), 160–76.

Van Zoonen, L. (2005) *Entertaining the Citizen*. London: Rowman & Littlefield.

Verbeek, P.-P. (2005) *What Things Do: Philosophical Reflections on Technology, Agency, and Design*. University Park, PA: Pennsylvania State University Press.

Vincent, D. (2011) 'China used prisoners in lucrative internet gaming work', *Guardian*, 25 May. http://www.guardian.co.uk/world/2011/may/25/china-prisoners-internet-gaming-scam (accessed June 2011).

Walther, B.K. (2005) 'Pervasive game-play: theoretical reflections and classifications'. www1.sdu.dk/Hum/bkw/walther-pg-article-06.pdf (accessed July 2012).

Wardrip-Fruin, N. and Harrigan, P. (2004) *First Person: New Media as Story, Performance, and Game*. Cambridge, MA: MIT Press.

Wellman, B. and Haythornthwaite, C. (eds) (2002) *The Internet in Everyday Life*. Oxford: Blackwell.

Williams, D. (n.d.) 'A brief social history of game play'. www.dmitriwilliams.com/williamssochist.doc (accessed 5 April 2011).

Williams, D. (2003) 'The video game lightning rod: constructions of a new media technology 1970–2000', *Information, Communication & Society* 6(4), 523–50.

Williams, D., Ducheneaut, N., Xiong, L., Yee, N. and Nickell, E. (2006) 'From tree house to barracks: the social life of guilds in World of Warcraft', *Games and Culture* 1(4), 338–61.

Williams, D., Kennedy, T.L.M. and Moore, R.J. (2011) 'Behind the avatar: the patterns, practices, and functions of role playing in MMOs', *Games and Culture* 6(2), 171–200.

Williams, R. (1991) 'Dreamworlds of consumption', in C. Mukerji and M. Schudson (eds) *Rethinking Popular Culture: Contemporary Perspectives in Culture Studies*. Berkeley, CA: University of California Press.

Winnicott, D. (1971) *Playing and Reality*. London: Tavistock Press.

Yee, N. (2006) 'The demographics, motivations and derived experiences of users of massively multi-user online graphical environments', *PRESENCE: Teleoperators and Virtual Environments* 15(3), 309–29.

Yee, N. (2009) 'Befriending ogres and wood-elves: relationship formation and the social architecture of Norrath', *Game Studies* 9(1).

Žižek, S. (2009) *First as Tragedy, Then as Farce*. London: Verso.

Zukin, S. (2004) *Point of Purchase: How Shopping Changed American Culture*. London: Routledge.

Games

Adventure (1975) Crowther, W.
Championship Manager (1992) Collyer, P. and O. Domark, UK
Computer Space (1971) Bushnell, N. Dabney, T. Nutting Associates
Counterstrike (1999) Le, M. and J. Cliffe, Valve Software
Crash Bash (2000) Vivendi Games, Sony Computer Entertainment
Dance Dance Revolution (1998) Konami
Dead or Alive 4 (2005) Team Ninja
Death Race (1976) Exidy
Defender (1980) Williams Electronics
Deus Ex (2000) Square Enix, Eidos Interactive
Doom (1994) id software
Dr Kawashimu's Brain Training: How Old is Your Brain? (2005) Nintendo
Donkey Kong (1981) Nintendo
ET: The Extra-Terrestrial (1982) Atari Corporation
EverQuest (1999) Sony Online Entertainment
Grand Theft Auto: San Andreas (2006) Rock Star Games
Half Life (1998) Sierra
Halo (2001) Bungie Software
Journey (2012) That Game Company
Legend of Zelda (1986) Nintendo
Lord of the Rings Online (2007) Turbine
Manhunt (2003) Rock Star
Mortal Kombat: Armageddon (2006) Just Games Interactive/Midway
Myst (1994) Cyan
Namco Museum: Volume One (1995)
Naughty One (1983) Holdco
Pac-Man (1980) Midway Games
Pong (1972) Atari Incorporated
Rayman (1995) Ubisoft
Resident Evil 5 (2009) Nintendo
Space Invaders (1978) Taito
Spacewar (1962) Russell, S.
Streetfighter 4 (2009) Capcom
Strip Poker (1983) Knightsoft
Super Mario 2: Yoshi's Island (1995)
Syberia (2002) Microids
Syberia II (2004) Microids
Tetris (1984) Pajtinov
Tomb Raider (1996) Core design/crystal dynamics

Ultima Online (1997) Garriott, R. Electronic Arts
URU: Ages beyond Myst (2003) Ubi-soft
World of Warcraft (2004) Blizzard
Zelda II: The Adventures of Link (1987) Nintendo
Zelda: Ocarina of Time (1998) Nintendo

Index

Abbate, J. 65
active participation 19–20
addiction 136, 137–8, 139
Adorno, T.W. 18–19, 32, 33, 125,
    170, 172
    and Horkheimer, M. 17–18
aesthetics 163–70
    ethics of selfhood 140
    of technology 66–7
    of variable maintenance 25–7
    see also art and artistic critique
    of capitalism
Altair 54, 55
ambivalence in gaming culture
    91–7
Andersen, C.U. 51, 173
Aoyama, Y. see Izushi, H.
arcade/gambling machines
    47–9
art and artistic critique of
    capitalism 27–9, 66, 159,
    175–87
    play 170–5
    transformation of computing
    61–9, 99–100, 171–5
astrology columns 18–19, 32, 33
Atari 56, 57, 102
authenticity 24, 30, 81–91
autonomy 23–4, 159–60
avatars 140–4, 146, 147, 151,
    155–6

Behrenshausen, B. 164–5
Bennerstedt, U.
    and Ivarsson, J. 143, 150, 151
    Linderoth, J. and 157

Bergson, H. 181
Boltanski, L. 2–3, 13, 35, 36, 153,
    174
    and Chiapello, E. 4–5, 12,
    22–3, 24, 25, 27–8, 29–30,
    66, 92, 96, 99, 159, 167–8
Bourdieu, P. 42, 71, 72, 73, 80,
    81–2, 85
brain training and brain age
    30–4

capitalism
    consequences of 98–100
    marketing strategies 119–20
    and subversion 121–2, 177
    see also art and artistic critique
    of capitalism
Carstens, A. and Beck, J. 25
cartridge-based systems 56, 57
Castells, M. 109
Castoriadis, C. 14
Castronova, E. 131, 156, 157
Cauldron 79
Championship Manager 111
Chapan, M. 5, 99, 54
childhood
    marketing strategies and
        technological
        empowerment 119–22
    social development 132–4
    and teenage culture 95–6
comic book art 112–14
Commodore 74–5, 76, 78–9
Commodore User (CU)
    (magazine) 78–9, 80, 84,
    90

communication channels 145–6, 147
communicative action and practice 16, 163–4
competitiveness 25
Computer Space 48, 71
Computer and Video Gaming (CVG) (magazine) 76–8, 84, 86–8, 89, 90–1, 93–4
Consalvo, M. 75, 88, 110, 112, 115–16
consumerism *see* art and artistic critique of capitalism; capitalism
Costa, N. 47–8
counter-culture (1960s) 27–8, 29, 55, 61–3, 64, 66
Crary, J. 46
Crash Bandicoot 121
Crawford, G. 111
culture
    and technology 111–18
    see also gaming culture, formation of
culture industry 17–19
    global 20–1
    new and old 34
cynicism 24, 96–7

Dance Dance Revolution (DDR) 164–5
De Prato, G. et al. 104–5, 110–11
'de-coupled' and 'naturalized' play 166–7
dependency 17, 18–19, 20–1
Deuze, M. 106
    et al. 57–8, 106–7, 108
'dialectic of invention' 54
    technology and 49–61
Digital Equipment Corporation (DEC) 55, 63
dis-identification 178, 181
discourse
    and identity 72–4
    and notion of gameplay 76–81, 84–91, 93–5, 167

dissensus 175–6, 182–3
dissonance 169–70
Dr Kawashima's Brain Train Program 30–3
Dyer-Witheford, N. and de Peuter, G. 11, 37, 48–9, 50, 57, 65, 98, 100, 110, 111–12, 123, 126

Ehrenreich, B. 24, 149
embodiment 82–3, 84, 164–6, 183–4, 185
employment *see* work
empowerment of children 120–2
end user license agreements (EULAs) 123–4
Europe 47, 58, 74, 110–11, 113–14, 154
EverQuest 140–1, 147

Farne, R. 45
Feenberg, A. 44–5, 66, 122
    and Freedman, J. 62
Foucault, M. 140, 154
fragmented self 23, 26, 27
Freiberger, P. and Swaine, M. 63, 64

gambling/arcade machines 47–9
gameplay 167–70, 184–5
    discourse and notion of 76–81, 84–91, 93–5, 167
    discovery/invention of 74–81
    ludefaction and diminution of 150–8
gamers *see* identity; self
games engines (SDKs) 103–6
games industry
    'crash' (1980s) 57–9, 59–61, 74
    global 101–9
Gamespot 171
gaming culture, formation of 70–4

authenticity 24, 30, 81–91
constitutive ambivalence 91–7
see also gameplay
gaming magazines 75–9, 80–1,
84–5, 86–9
Gee, J.P. 183–5
global culture industry 20–1
global games industry 101–9
globalization and cultures of
production 109–18
'Go' 44–5
gold-farmers 156–7
Golumbia, D. 138, 139, 145, 147,
156, 158
Göncü, A. and Perone, A. 45
governance, lack of 151–4
Gregersen, A. 83
grinding 139, 145, 151
guilds 148, 150
Gutman, D 59–60

Habermas, J. 15–16, 17, 18, 53,
142, 143, 153
habitus 72, 73, 81–2, 83, 85,
185
hacking 122–3
'hippy hackers' 63
and modding 123–7
Heeks, R. 156, 157
Heilbroner, R. 30
Higinbotham, W. 49–50
Hill, J.A. 73, 95, 120
history 38–40
first computer game 48–9
of play 43–4, 45–8
revival of play 20–1, 40–9,
67–8
technology and dialectic of
invention 49–61
home/small computers 62–4,
74–5, 76, 121
Honneth, A. 130, 132–4, 140
honour/respect 139–40
Huhtamo, E. 38, 47
Huizinga, J. 43–4
Humphreys, S. 144, 152–3, 154

identity 86, 88, 92–3, 96–7
child-directed marketing
strategies 120
dis-identification 178, 181
discourse and 72–4
see also self
'imagined communities' 15, 36
independent development *vs*
standardization 106–7
interface design 65, 103, 118,
122–3
Izushi, H.
and Aoyama, Y. 60, 75, 105,
112–13, 114, 115
Aoyama, Y. and 48, 106,
116–17

Japan
arcade gaming 47, 48–9
and crash of US gaming
industry 60, 112
globalization of gaming
industry 110–11, 114, 115–17
manga art 112, 13
modernization of 44–5
Johns, J. 50, 110, 116
Journey 168–9, 179–81

Kawashima, R. 30–3
Kendrick, L. 43
Kerr, A. 11, 106, 110, 117
Kirkpatrick, G. 53, 65, 72, 96,
103, 120, 164, 165, 175
Kline, S. et al. 83, 95, 99–100,
102, 115, 119, 121

Lash, S. and Lury, C. 1, 2, 20–1,
34, 99, 101, 119, 126, 173,
174
Latin America 114
laughter 181–2
learning 185–6
Leary, T. 65
Linderoth, J. 185
and Bennerstedt, U. 157
ludefaction 7, 131, 150–8

magazines 75–9, 80–1, 84–5,
    86–9, 93–4
Malliet, S. and Meyer, G.
    49–50, 51, 56, 57–8, 104
manga art 112–13
Marcuse, H. 62, 66, 118–19
marketing strategies 119–20
Marx, K. 16
massive multi-player on-line
    games (MMPGs) 128–31
    limitations of engineered
        sociability 139–50
    ludefaction and diminution of
        gameplay 150–8
    recognition-theoretical
        perspective 131–9
media
    importance of 16–17
    print 15–17, 154
Microsoft 102
middleware (SDKs) 103–6
military uses 49–51
Miyamoto, S. 83, 113, 117
modding 123–7
modernity 44–5
Montfort, N. and Bogost, I. 57

'naturalized' and 'de-coupled'
    play 166–7
The Naughty One 89–90, 161
Nelson, T. 63
networked computing 64–5, 118
networked organizations 23–4
networked society 24–5, 27, 92,
    150, 177
Neville, R. 29
Nieborg, D.B.
    and Hermes, J. 36
    and van der Graaf, S. 105, 125
Nielsen, H.S. 83, 166–7, 183
Nintendo
    cartoon art 112
    child-directed marketing
        strategy 119
    Dr Kawashima's Brain Train
        Program 30–3

globalization of gaming
    industry 102, 115
hacking/modding 122, 123
'play revival' 60, 70
technological innovations 52,
    56, 58–9

Occupy movement 177

panopticon 154–5
Pearce, C. 132, 146–7
phenakisticon 155, 158
play 34–5
    definitions of 41–3
    history of 43–4, 45–8
    modernity and 44–5
    revival of 20–1, 40–9, 67–8
    work and 22, 25–6, 29–31,
        66, 67, 156
playability 77, 78, 81
policing 152
print media 15–17, 154
public sphere 15–16, 154

Rancière, J. 162–3, 175–9, 189
recognition/recognition-
    theoretical perspective
    26–7, 91–2, 131–9, 150–1,
    153–6
repetition ('grinding') 139, 145,
    151, 166
Resident Evil 4 184
Resident Evil 5 166–7
resistance/subversion 118–27,
    177
    counter-culture (1960s) 27–8,
        29, 55, 61–3, 64, 66
respect/honour 139–40
'role' players (RPers) and non
    RPers ('normal' players)
    137–9
Ruch, A. 152, 153, 154
Russell, S. 50

Sassen, S. 108, 109–10, 112
Scheff, D. 52, 59, 60, 122

Sega 48, 93–4, 102–3, 114, 119, 121
self
  and avatars 140–4, 146, 147, 155–6
  ethics and aesthetics 140
  fragmented 23, 26, 27
  modern sense of 16–17
  'streamlined self' 21–7
  see also identity
Sennett, R. 22–3
sexism 89–91
Shadowfire 79
Shinkle, E. 165, 167
small/home computers 62–4, 74–5, 76, 121
social conflicts 36–7
social constructionist perspective 52–3
'social forums' 145–6, 147
social relationships 134–6, 157–8
  childhood development 132–4
  engineered, limitations of 139–40
social theory 14–21
  and critique 27–37
  'streamlined self' 21–7
software development kits (SDKs) 103–6
Sony 102, 103, 121, 123
Space Invaders 50
Spacewar! 50, 51, 52, 55, 64
Square/Square Enix 110–11
Stafford, B. 45
standardization vs independent development 106–7
'streamlined self' 21–7
Strip Poker 90
subversion see resistance
Suits, B. 41
Swalwell, M. viii
symbolic meanings 16

Taylor, C. 2, 15
Taylor, T.L. 128, 141, 156
technology 98–101

aesthetics of 66–7
and dialectic of invention 49–61
games industry 101–9
globalization and cultures of production 109–18
power and resistance 118–27
print media 15–17, 154
Thompson, J.B. 15, 16–17, 82
Turkle, S. 134, 150, 178
Turner, F. 50, 54, 55, 63, 64, 122

United Kingdom (UK) 58–9, 74–5, 112, 113, 115, 117
United States (US)
  counter-culture (1960s) 27–8, 29, 55, 61–3, 64, 66
  crash of gaming industry 57–8, 59–61, 74, 112
  gaming magazines 75
  globalization of gaming industry 110–11, 115–16
  history of gaming machines 47, 56
  military 49–51

van Dijck, J. 124–5
Vanard, K. 171
visual computing 114, 118–19

Weizenbaum, J. 51
Williams, D. 57, 86
  et al. 134, 135, 136, 137, 148, 150
Williams, R. 46
work
  employment conditions 23, 107–8, 117–18
  and play 22, 25–6, 29–30, 66, 67, 156
  transformation of 28–9, 62
World of Warcraft (WoW) 139, 145, 147, 149, 157

Yee, N. 134, 136, 137–8, 141, 145

Žižek, S. 33–4